# MAKING RESIDENTIAL CARE WORK

# Dartington Social Research Series

# Making Residential Care Work

STRUCTURE AND CULTURE IN CHILDREN'S HOMES

Elizabeth Brown
Roger Bullock
Caroline Hobson
Michael Little
*Dartington Social Research Unit*

Published by
Ashgate Publishing Limited
Gower House
Croft Road
Aldershot
Hants GU11 3HR
England

Ashgate Publishing Company
Old Post Road
Brookfield
Vermont 05036
USA

**British Library Cataloguing in Publication Data**
Making residential care work : structure and culture in
   children's home. - (Dartington social research series)
   1.Children - Institutional care - Great Britain
   2.Institutional care - Great Britain - Evaluation
   I.Brown, Elizabeth
   362.7'32

**Library of Congress Catalog Card Number:** 98-70907


ISBN 1 84014 499 8 (Hbk)
ISBN 1 84014 457 2 (Pbk)


Printed and bound in Great Britain by
Biddles Ltd, Guildford and King's Lynn

# Contents

# Index of diagrams and tables

# Acknowledgements

This study has been prepared by members of the Dartington Social Research Unit, Elizabeth Brown, Roger Bullock, Caroline Hobson and Michael Little. It would not have been possible without the active support of colleagues in the Research Unit, Debbie Doyle, Daniel Gooch, Heather Leitch, Yvonne McCann, Kevin Mount and Oliver Noakes and the help of several local authorities and voluntary and independent organisations. We are extremely grateful, too, to the staff and children who helped us with our task: we were welcomed into the homes, often at moments of uncertainty and anxiety and it is only through their perseverance with our tedious questioning and requests that we were able to learn about the structures and cultures that prevailed.

The research was funded by the Department of Health and we would like to thank the Directors of Research and Development, Professor Sir Michael Peckham and Professor John Swales. The study would not have been possible without the assistance of the Social Care Division and the Social Services Inspectorate and we are grateful to Dr. Valerie Brasse, Norman Duncan, Ted Hillier, Elizabeth Johnson, Sir Herbert Laming, Tom Luce, John Rowlands and Wendy Rose. We have also benefited greatly from the research management undertaken by Dr. Carolyn Davies.

We also wish to thank colleagues in universities, local authorities, voluntary agencies and members of the Dartington Unit who have advised, assisted and commented on our work. Particular thanks go to Lesley Archer, David Berridge, Brenda Bullock, Leslie Hicks, Barbara Kahan, Spencer Millham, Roy Parker, Ian Sinclair and Richard Whipp.

# 1 Introduction

This introduction is being written in the lobby of a hotel, the venue of a conference on the strengths and weaknesses of residential care. The hotel is in England, although from the inside, in a quiet corner away from staff and residents whose voice or dress might give something away, it could as easily be in the United States, Australia or even the Far East. By the reckoning of all the delegates, it is a good hotel. Why should this be? Perhaps it is because of a key individual, the manager or chef, neither of whom anyone present has seen. Perhaps it is the decor, a triumph for the affective neutrality that appeals to tourists as much as to social workers. Possibly the level of technology employed here can provide an explanation, the effortless check-in, the 20 channel television or the mini-bar that registers purchases the moment they leave the fridge. Whatever the causes, the hotel certainly works, convincing even the most analytically minded researcher that it is provided for him or her alone and that no-one else has ever occupied the bed that beckons each evening.

When studying residential institutions, the immediate ports of call are the surface features, the leadership, the fabric and the resources just mentioned. Indeed, because residence is about people, it is their behaviour that comes to obsess. 'Oh, she is wonderful, it's such a lovely children's home' or 'Oh, how awful, I don't know why the staff put up with it.' 'If only we could transfer the first manager to the second home, all would be well.' After visiting several hundred residential institutions over the last 30 years we at Dartington have come to conclude that there are deeper explanations for the varying performance of residential institutions, particularly those designed for children.

The publication *Residential Care for Children: A review of the*

1

*research** emphasised the difficulties of establishing a unified theory of residential care. Problems arise by virtue of the fact that there is no one task to be achieved and no single method of producing good results. A residential approach may be perfectly valid theoretically or practically but if the context is wrong then the effort is wasted. Nonetheless, what is agreed by most professionals is that to get a high quality service, the different aspects of residential care have to be complementary. Terms such as 'concordance', 'balance' and 'congruence' would form the building blocks of any discourse on residential care.

It goes without saying that looking after children well for 24 hours a day, seven days a week requires homes to be well run. They have to be properly staffed, effectively administered and free from destructive conflicts. Few would doubt that there are useful lessons for managers to learn from organisation and management theory - it clearly helps if aims are well thought out, roles clearly articulated and communication effective. Recent child protection inquiries have revealed, however, that though these may be necessary conditions for a high quality service, they are certainly not sufficient. Behind seemingly ordered façades, neglect and abuse can thrive. So an additional requirement is for regimes to be based on welfare principles, such as those that underpin the *Children Act,* 1989 and for the methods used in the home to be right for the needs of the children.

In any scrutiny of residential care, it is necessary to bear in mind the possibilities of discord in some part of the system, no matter how pleasant things may seem on the surface. It is very easy for relationships between the parts to change and go off balance. The child care literature abounds with illustrations of seemingly ridiculous anomalies. Berridge in *Children's Homes* described a home that changed its function to care for older teenagers but failed to adapt the furniture. Rows of feet hanging from the ends of bunk-beds were his lasting memory of that establishment. Less dramatic, in this study a home called Blue retained aims and objectives based on its earlier work with long stay children moving on to adoption or independence. These proved inappropriate for the home's later role of caring for a wide mix of children for shorter periods. As in many of the homes studied, the

---

* Since there is such a broad literature on children's residential care, footnote references to books and articles have been avoided. Where a reference is mentioned the full title is given in the text. A fuller explanation of the literature is given in Appendix 1.

chasm between function in theory and function in practice leaves staff bemused and anxious.

Given these possibilities, several questions arise. The key issues for both policy makers and professionals are, who needs residential care? followed by, for what reason, what type, for how long and with what other services? In the process of considering such questions, the different functions of residential care become apparent and interventions are seen in the context of their relevance to different points in children's care careers. The term 'career' incorporates two aspects of children's experiences: the first is those decisions young people make (or parents make on their behalf) which affect future life chances; the second is the response of agencies and the decisions they make on the child's behalf. By understanding the interaction between them it is often possible to predict with reasonable accuracy long term outcomes in children's lives. Such a perspective helps to link the needs of the child, the service delivered as well as desired and actual outcomes. It also helps identify the value-added aspects of services, along with contributions made by families, schools and communities to children's welfare. Residential care is viewed less as a conjuror's 'black box' inducing change in the individuals within it and more as one of a number of interventions that may be applied at different times. One effect of this approach is to make redundant choices between welfare and control or treatment and containment.

This line of inquiry leads to further important questions about residential care. Are the right children in the homes? How is an appropriate intervention to be selected? How can care of the highest quality be ensured? How can outcomes be evaluated? It would be impossible for a single research project to answer all of these questions and different studies are needed for each. This particular study of structure and cultures makes a contribution to the questions of quality and outcomes and, in doing so, complements other projects in a research programme into residential care commissioned by the Department of Health. The work by Sinclair and Gibbs, *Quality of Care in Children's Homes* and by Whitaker, Archer and Hicks, *The Prevailing Cultures and Staff Dynamics in Children's Homes* deal with similar questions to this study but adopt a slightly different focus. The first seeks general patterns from a comparison of the structural features and children's adaptations in 48 homes: the second gives a very detailed analysis of staff cultures but concentrates on general processes rather than on particular establishments. Other projects in the programme, such as Whipp's work on the management of homes, explore some of the related issues just discussed. Recent publications from other sources are also relevant. Several publications from the Department's *Support Force for Children's Residential Care* provide managers with methodologies and instruments for assessing the needs of the children and the *Looking After Children* materials enable professionals to evaluate the outcomes of the service provided. The links between these seemingly disparate activities are apparent in the overview of the research programme. This publication is similar to the two so-called 'Pink Books' (*Social Work Decisions in Child Care* and *Patterns and Outcomes in Child Placement*) and to *Child Protection: Messages from Research*, the 'Blue Book'.

## The special focus of this study

What does this study seek to contribute? The terms 'structure' and 'culture' are hardly new and some observers might argue that the plethora of institutional research in the 1960s left little else to say. But, as will be explained, the context of children's homes today is very different. It is unlikely that the adult regimes described by Goffman and Sykes, with their violent and exploitative undercultures, can be considered to reflect life in community homes looking after children in need in the 1990s.

Yet all is not well in residential child care. Even if the terrible abuse revelations of recent years are excluded, few local authorities and voluntary agencies are happy with the service they provide. Despite numerous training initiatives, such as those by the Gatsby Project in conjunction with the Open University and by Caldecott College, helpful publications such as Volume Four of the *Children Act* Guidance and Kahan's book *Growing Up in Groups*; and despite increasingly generous staffing quotas and salary arrangements, it is generally agreed that the service remains of variable quality. Some excellent work is taking place but the general picture is one of mediocrity. It was disappointing to find in the application of the *Looking After Children* materials similar shortfalls in children's health, education, family and social relationships as had been found 25 years earlier in the research on approved schools for *After Grace-Teeth*. A few homes seem to fare worse than this: they teeter on the brink of disaster and staff seem preoccupied, trying to keep the lid on a boiling pot. This is not helped by staff fears of abuse accusations, press reports of tearaways crashing cars or teenage prostitutes 'working from home'. As a manager at the Caldecott Community expressed it in *A Life without Problems?*, 'Sometimes I feel like an NCO at Ypres. I just lead them (the staff) over the top to slaughter.' The decline of belief in residential approaches makes it increasingly difficult to convince staff and social workers that an important service specified in the *Children Act*, 1989 is being provided.

But few homes actually fit stereotypes, whether good or bad. This study, based on nine unremarkable establishments, uncovered great variety both of practice approaches and quality of care. Some homes clearly worked well and were undoubtedly good places. Others muddled along, achieving moderately but doing no harm, whilst one establishment lurched from crisis to crisis. Both this research from Dartington and the recent work of Sinclair and Gibbs have sought to explain these differences quantitatively and have highlighted the variables, such as size, certain aspects of staff performance and children's backgrounds that correlate with success. But, even given this knowledge, it is still difficult to link results to policy, since an unsatisfactory and insecure home is unlikely to welcome the results of research with open arms.

It may be irritating that factors such as the qualifications of staff or the condition of buildings do not in themselves correlate with good homes, but this is undeniably so. Every research project undertaken in this area has found examples of untrained carers working in dilapidated surroundings doing an excellent job. But neither should it be concluded that training or buildings are irrelevant. Obviously, people are likely to do a better job with greater confidence if taught how to do it and are more likely to be content if the ambience is pleasant. There is a danger of a circular argument that runs as follows: how can we identify a good home? - the staff and children are happy and know what the home is about. When will staff and residents be happy and know what the home is about?- when they live in a good home. A point of entry to break the circle is necessary if improving strategies are to be implemented.

One solution to this problem is to use independent outcome measures of what is good and bad for children. These will show what works, using indicators unconnected to the variables under scrutiny. Chapters Eight and Nine of this report do this with outcomes for homes themselves and then for the children. Another is to adopt an alternative explanation based on a more interactive model where risk and protective factors impact in a causal chain. Another is to use global concepts, such as ethos or culture, which combine variables in some way. Given that individual factors do not correlate with success as frequently as might be expected, some scrutiny of staff and child cultures is indicated. A novel feature of this research is its focus on individual homes and the charting of changes in their fortunes over the period of a year. As far as is known, before the current Department of Health research programme, no study has ever done this, despite the well established fact that homes go through good and bad patches. Again, it is to be hoped that the messages from this part of the project will help managers remedy unsatisfactory situations and raise standards.

Structures and cultures are important for the welfare of children because the values which they sanction influence individual staff and child responses and collective behaviour. Unless managers and inspectors understand the forces shaping residential life, professionals will face continuing difficulties in affecting what goes on in homes. Children's behaviours that worry adults - swearing, smoking, sex, bullying, running away *et cetera* - are largely controlled by the informal rules enshrined in these cultures and by the attitudes and actions necessary for staff and children to be popular (or unpopular) with their peers. It is salutary to be reminded that despite all the statistical evidence about smoking and health and all the educational programmes this has led to, there is still no reasonable explanation as to why so many staff and residents in community homes smoke.

The particular contribution of this study is the child culture and its interaction with that of the staff. While one cannot understand the former without considering the latter, the connection between the two is by no means fixed and a lot can be done to promote healthy relationships. Given the difficult role of residential care, apathy and alienation among children and staff are always likely responses but they should not be assumed as inevitable. Research shows that alternatives are possible. This and other projects will lead to the development of a practice tool that will enable managers to assess the quality of care in children's homes and gain a better understanding of the complex processes that have been described. They should also delineate a series of interventions that can be applied to improve matters in homes facing difficulties.

## The changing context of residential care

Before venturing into the inner worlds of residence, it is useful to explore the wider context of residential child care. It provides an important part of Part III services specified in the *Children Act*, 1989 but its uses for children in care or accommodation have changed. The most notable feature is a marked decline. The numbers of children (under 18) in residential establishments in England and Wales for welfare, criminal or special education reasons fell by 47% to 32,900 in the 20 years between 1971 and 1991, the dates of two accurate surveys by Moss in 1975 and by Gooch in 1991. The fall in the numbers living in children's homes has been even greater and, as figures in Chapter Four show, on March 31st 1996, there were under 7,000 children in these placements in England and Wales, a drop of 70% since 1971. But against this, it is important to emphasise that because ever fewer young people enter residential care before they enter secondary schools, the potential for long stays is reduced, and figures for the annual throughput of children will be greater. In a study by Dartington of all admissions to residential care in one county, it was found that twice as many children were admitted to residential care over a year as were resident at any one time. Some children were admitted more than once and one emergency unit averaged nine annual admissions per bed.

It is clear that a sizeable proportion of adolescents being looked after are still likely to have a residential experience. Because of practice changes over the last decade, the figure is less than the 80% found for those admitted to care over the age of ten in the *Lost in Care* cohort studied in the early 1980s; in *Going Home* the figure is 60%. Moreover, as Cliffe and Berridge report in *Closing Children's Homes*, those local authorities that have stopped providing children's residential care, such as Solihull and Warwickshire, have found that for a proportion (some 10-15%) of adolescents there is no viable alternative. Similarly, following the application of a Dartington planning tool called *Matching*

*Needs and Services,* an analysis of referrals to several social services departments identified a group of children whose needs were best met by residential care, although not always of the type available. But despite this continuing demand, further decline seems likely as discriminating purchasers seek value for money and cheaper alternatives.

Social workers' attitudes to residential care and the implementation of other child care policies, such as bail support for offenders, must affect what happens in the homes. It can hardly boost the morale of the residential sector constantly to be seen as a 'last resort'. The growing tendency to choose residence late in children's care careers would suggest that the children will be older (although it may surprise some to learn that 17% of those included in this study were under the age of ten) and that they will present complex and challenging needs. Individually, the young people are probably no more difficult than their predecessors 20 years ago but today the most challenging come together in small groups with few straight forward cases to ease the burden for hard pressed staff. Dartington's study of approved school boys in the late 1960s, for example, found that 30% had serious psychological problems while the remainder could be categorised as socialised delinquents. They were certainly anti-social and emotionally deprived but they posed relatively little trouble to staff. Few of these young men would be in residential establishments today and they are an example of the exodus of the marginal from residential care.

Care must be taken when generalising about residential services. Any search for single-issue explanations of developments in services must account for the revivals of the 1970s as well as the decline of the 1980s. Neither should the fact that children in residential care undoubtedly have complex needs be confused with myths that they are all delinquent or all victims of sexual abuse. Nonetheless, over a dozen separate trends within the residential sector as a whole are identified. These are as true of public schools and hospitals as they are of children's homes and include: the replacement of single-sex establishments by homes that are co-educational but which, in practice, are dominated by boys; the increasing age of residents at entry; more young people with health problems, behaviour disorders and disabilities; greater racial and ethnic mix; larger catchment areas, raising problems for educational continuity and contact with home; more provision by private agencies;

less specialisation by sector with a resulting mix of needs in each
establishment; assessment by need criteria rather than social role
categories, such as disabled or special educational needs; a more
generalist service; shorter stays; rising costs; more concerns about rights
and protection; and, further reductions in the size of units and in the
numbers accommodated by the system. Naturally, the factors that
explain changes in the use of private boarding schools, schools for
children with special educational needs and penal institutions may be
different from those that affect children's homes but in each of these
sectors, viable alternatives have been created. Even in the sectors
primarily concerned with the delinquent and disruptive adolescent, the
emergence of a coherent system of state-sponsored social work has been
of major importance, although there is still considerable dependency on
residence as a last resort.

The *Children Act*, 1989 echoes previous attempts, such as the
*Wagner Report* of 1988, to shed the 'last resort' image and ensure that
residential care is integral to children's services. It remains a perfectly
valid service that should be used as a 'positive choice'. It should be
sufficiently attractive to young people for them to request it if they so
wish. The strengths of the best residential approaches have been laid
out in several Dartington papers and it is encouraging that several
recent studies of teenagers in community homes have found that many
young people speak favourably about their experiences. All children in
need have a right to those services that can be shown to be in their best
interest. Sadly, some residential care falls short of providing this but, as
this and other studies show, some children's homes work well.

This chapter began with some observations about a hotel, a place
where adults and children understand the rules, boundaries and implicit
relationships. It might be instructive to end with a reference to *Lord of
the Flies*, Golding's novel about children left to their own devices on a
desert island. Whether cultures emerged around the central characters
Ralph and Jack is difficult to assess but it is possible to predict with
greater certainty that had they not been rescued, additional fatalities
would have been inevitable. Children's homes mostly aim to provide
more than the anti-septic order of a hotel; they try, and usually succeed,
in avoiding the degeneration evident in *Lord of the Flies*. Somewhere
between the two lies a pattern of structure and culture that best suits

the needs of different groups of children; such is the pursuit of this book.

# 2 Structure, cultures and outcomes

Residential care is more than the bricks and mortar of the building. It is much more than the people who live and work within the institutional walls. Even the additional focus on the social relationships between staff and residents is unlikely to capture the full flavour of life within a residential community. Commentators have tried to separate out the constituent parts of residence. Many talk of the structure of institutions, which is taken to include their fabric and, where they are articulated, their aims and objectives. Some refer to this as the 'formal' world of the home, usually meaning that which is tangible or written down. In contrast, there is the 'informal' world - the talk, smells, interactions and ether which, for a variety of reasons that will be explained, comes to be defined as 'culture' in this study.

The dimensions of formal, informal and structure are not easily adapted for scientific study. Certain aspects, such as the number of beds occupied, the staff-child ratio or the rate of running away, to name but a few, are easily measured. But other features seem more the preserve of the writer than the scientist. To read the *Hothouse Society* with its chapters on 'a place in the sun', 'this tiny universe' and 40 pages on sex; to consider Goffman's sources in *Asylums* or to glance at the title of *Neill! Neill! Orange Peel!* is to know that institutions attract as many expressive writers as they do obsessive researchers.

But for all their richness, the expressives fail to define the ethereal and, therefore, fail to show how the tacit, informal and cultural - depending on the writer's preferred terminology - might be used to predict change within a home or the quality of life of those within it. Moreover, it is difficult to find in the literature a general theory about those aspects of residence which resist measurement, like the informal world. As a consequence, ideas seldom travel across institutional contexts. So Goffman's fascinating insight into 'stashing', carrying one's personal possessions around the mental hospital, or Lambert and Millham's captivating observation on the need of public school boys to remain in the 'closed world' of the institution, often at some cost to their happiness and dignity, have little relevance elsewhere, particularly to the small children's home which lies at the heart of this study.

So it was with mixed feelings that a challenge to look again at the 'formal and informal worlds of staff and children in residential care' - the working title for the project at its inception - was accepted. Would there be anything new to say about the subject and could the ideas be adapted to the rigorous scientific scrutiny required of contemporary child care research? Where encouragement was to be found, it emerged from the increasing literature on culture within organisations produced by management analysts and not from the sparse literature on residential care available in the last 20 years. As will be seen, the former prompted a look at change within institutions which, in turn, shaped other ideas upon which the study is based.

## The changed context of research on residential care

Before defining the terms used in this book and a set of theories about what makes for a good residential home (that is one which achieves positive outcomes for its children) it is necessary to consider the changed context within which residential care research operates. When A.S. Neill wrote about Summerhill, institutions were viewed as fixed and their residents as potential subjects of change. It was common in the 1960s to ask 'what happens in the black box?' referring to life within the children's home or approved school which had the potential to alter the trajectories of the children, whether those in care or juvenile delinquents. Goffman painted a picture of a person going into a mental hospital, experiencing a regime largely unchanged from that in place a century before and by becoming an inmate, setting in motion a steady process of deterioration which might take years to complete.

Such a perspective worked well with a largely unchanging institution; indeed, it was the apparent steadiness of the inmates' environment that made residential settings such a popular area for study among other social scientists in the two decades following the Second World War. Variables could be controlled and large-scale studies undertaken at minimum cost. This produced a rather static picture and, from a reading of the studies 20 years later, Sykes's prisons, Goffman's asylums and Lambert's public schools seem remarkable for the consistency of their service. When asked whether he was worried about the prospects of change engendered by the changing political climate of the mid 1960s, the headmaster of a great Catholic public school answered calmly, 'Oh no, if necessary we will move. We have moved three times: first in 1093, again in 1340 and we came here in 1850. If necessary we will move again'.

In fact, the assumption that institutions were unchanging was mistaken. What is remarkable about the public schools is their ability to adapt to new market conditions. The asylums that so mesmerised Goffman have mostly been closed in the 30 years that followed the publication of his book (the two events are not connected). Only prisons have survived in anything like their former state and, even here, public concern about rising crime has not dissuaded even the most punitive of politicians from sanctioning the abandonment of archaic traditions such as 'slopping out'.

Change in the residential sector has not been confined to reduced volume of provision. The Approved Schools studied by Dartington in the 1960s became Community Homes with Education in the 1970s, with a few achieving complete metamorphosis by turning into therapeutic communities. Of the 20 children's homes studied by Berridge in 1984, 16 have closed, two are about to close and the remaining two have changed their function. In the nine homes scrutinised in this book, it will be seen that periodic changes in purpose and function have become a standard feature of provision. Indeed, as the later chapters demonstrate, most change is positive; the ability of a service to adapt to the needs of different groups of children can be viewed as a virtue.

So recent years have witnessed considerable flux in children's homes. But what about the residents? Not only are they getting older and presenting more complex problems; many of them do not get a chance to be changed by the institutional experience. Out of a cumulative sample of 462 children looked after in 1993, as reported in the *Going Home* (2nd Edition) study, 106 were first placed in a children's home. However, 19 of them had left, either returning home or moving to another placement, within a week of arrival and 56 departed within the next month. So much for the career of the inmate, as Goffman puts it. 'Saturday job' would seem more apt than 'career' and 'guest' more appropriate than 'inmate'.

This study started with the formal and informal worlds of children's homes, seeking to define for managers with little experience of residence what the world-weary residential worker sees in a home. It quickly became a pre-occupation with change and, later still, with predicting change in homes. Thus, while some of the terms, ideas, concepts and theories informing the book are long standing, the context to which they are applied is new.

## Structure and culture defined

This research began with a language borrowed from earlier Dartington and other research studies of residence. There, a distinction has been made between the formal order of children's homes, comprising goals, roles, control and authority, and the informal system of values and norms of behaviour which are not prescribed by the goals of the institution. These latter rules (or norms) were explored by asking questions such as 'what behaviour makes you popular or unpopular with other children?'. It was expected that in all residential establishments there would be unwritten regulations determining acceptable behaviour and attitudes among colleagues and peers, together with informal sanctions for defaulters. This way of understanding the complex world of residence was then applied to both staff and children.

In the present project, it soon became clear that this approach was no longer adequate. Problems of definition soon became apparent. The words 'formal' and 'informal' were not sufficient to cope with the range of actions of which residents and staff were capable. Taking children to school might be thought of as 'formal', but what about being nice to them on the way? Turning a blind eye to a child smoking a cigarette could be classified as 'informal', but with older adolescents who choose to take up their legal right to smoke, the behaviour becomes formalised.

A lack of clarity between 'formal' and 'informal' would have been manageable were the staff and children in residential homes to act as separate groups. In Sykes's prison and Goffman's asylum, both of which housed over 1,000 inmates, the staff behaved very differently from the residents and each group adopted recognisable and distinctive rules and customs. Presumably there were exceptions - deviants within the deviant group - but these are not reported. A look at a small children's home with 10 beds watched over by a dozen or more staff does not immediately reveal such an obvious group dynamic and the extended analysis afforded to research was seldom sufficient to uncover a discrete child culture. So while the words 'formal' and 'informal' captured the focus of this study, they were not sufficiently distinctive to convey the complexities of life within a contemporary residential centre for children or to chart the changes that take place within its walls.

In searching for alternative definitions, there was a determination to maintain the mix which has been the hallmark of theory and concepts used in previous Dartington studies. So, there was a place for structural functional ideas, interested in how a home is organised and what it is intended to do. Similarly, consideration was to be given to informal processes within the homes, a perspective that had already been informed by the work of social psychologists, not least Argyle, and sociologists like Thomas, Mead and Whyte, concerned with the way people understand the world around them. A pre-occupation with symbols, such as 'the best room in the home' - an example of a perspective used by residents to make sense of everyday interaction - has led this way of working to be known as 'symbolic interactionism'. It was also important to draw upon the even more strangely named 'hermeneutic tradition', which not only deals with the meaning that individuals attach to objects and events but also considers the subjective processes by which people reflect, interpret and adapt behaviours accordingly.

Applying these ideas to the early findings from visits to the nine homes which are the subjects of this study, signalled the importance of two concepts. The first is *structure*, meaning here the written, formally agreed institutionalised arrangements which influence behaviour. The second is *culture*, defined in the Oxford English Dictionary as 'the customs, civilisation and achievements of a particular time or people'. In anthropological literature, culture is frequently explained in terms of the ether or the space between matter which is unexplained or inexplicable. This resonated with the original aims of the study to understand how experienced social work managers 'know' how a children's home is operating; they would say, 'it is in the ether'. The task of the research has been to explain as much of the ether or culture as is possible.

The starting point had to be the structure, those aspects of homes which could be directly observed. From the perspective of sociologists who look for the functions of a society's organisations, this would include the mechanisms by which an institution achieves its goals and the relationships between its different components. Who takes responsibility for the children going to school? Do the residential social workers, field workers, teachers and parents work together for the child's welfare? This way of understanding residential communities has been used in previous studies and is more fully described in one of Dartington's earliest publications, *A Manual to the Sociology of the School*. Becker captures the idea of structure (in the context of social relations) when he talks of 'an orderly arrangement of social relations' and 'a continuing arrangement of kinds of people governed by a concept of proper behaviour in their relations with each other'. His definition will be the one used in this study.

Culture is more resistant to definition. A group of sociologists and psychologists working in the early part of this century became interested in the symbols people use in their interactions with each other. Their disciples included the sociologist Becker who refers to conventional understandings shared by the participants of a society, which is reasonably helpful. Another was Gouldner who was more precise in his conception, viewing culture as the perceptions and behaviour which arise in response to a problem encountered by a group. So, faced with a common task, do staff in a children's home respond as a group or do they react individually? This view of culture fitted with early findings about the way the residential centres in this study were operating. In some establishments, a culture clearly in tune with the aims of the home was manifest, whereas elsewhere the predominant culture undermined the manager's objectives for individual children. In other homes, there was no obvious culture among staff and, as later chapters in this book reveal, it was rarer for children than staff to respond to problems as a group.

Culture defined in this way concurred with colleagues at the University of York working on *Prevailing Cultures and Staff Dynamics in Children's Homes*. Whitaker, Archer and Hicks rest their study on organisation psychology, particularly the work of Schein and social psychologists such as Argyle. The York team have integrated ideas on culture and group dynamics within the small company of staff in the majority of residential homes. Their analysis complements that offered in this book, certainly in the way it suggests that the culture can be transferred from one place to another and possibly in the way it breaks down the components of cultures in residential centres.

The terms 'structure' and 'culture' helped to differentiate between aspects of life within a children's home; for example, in separating the aim of providing a child with a good education from the value attached to schooling by the staff. But to explain how children's homes change and why some lurch from crisis to crisis while others remain relatively tranquil required further analysis.

## Societal, formal and belief goals

To explore change, it was found necessary to consider three aspects of the structure of children's homes. Three types of goal were identified. The first is *societal*, which concerns the goals and aspects of structure laid down or implied by law or public expectation. The second is *formal*, which covers the local adaptation of these ideas by managers and their implementation in practice. The third is *belief* which reflects the underlying beliefs and values of managers and staff.

It soon became clear that, in some homes, there were conflicting forces within the structure of the home. As all were operating within the framework of the *Children Act*, 1989, their societal goals were constant throughout the study. But the adaptation of these ideas *in situ* by managers, the formal goals of the home, varied considerably from place to place. The third type of goal, reflected in the underlying beliefs of managers was revealed by their style of interaction with colleagues and children and by their answers to questions about why they were involved in the job and what they were trying to achieve for the children.

In some homes, the research found considerable concordance between societal, formal and belief goals and some consistency in response to tasks or problems over time, the definition of culture adopted for this study. For example, in Cyan, a unit in a therapeutic community for long separated children, the formal goals were clear: to offer a safe environment within which individual and group therapy and education could take place. As the home was clearly integral to the range of Part III services which a local authority would want to have available for children in need, formal and societal goals were concordant. Furthermore, interviews with the unit manager in which she explained her beliefs about difficult children revealed not only an understanding of the Act and the principles upon which therapeutic communities operate but also a deep commitment to the children and to advancing knowledge about their difficulties. Any scrutiny of her behaviour and talk showed that these beliefs were heartfelt. Several visits were made to the unit over the 12 months of the study and each visit reached the same conclusions. The goals were concordant and consistent.

This could not be said for other homes in the study. As later chapters reveal, it was not uncommon to find managers who were hazy about the societal goals - as manifest by a poor understanding of the *Children Act,* 1989 or a failure to know that Volume Four, the accompanying Guidance on residential care, existed - and unclear about the formal goals of their home. In such circumstances, beliefs can be reduced to 'making sure I get through the day not too battle scarred'. Unsurprisingly, consistency in such settings was rare; goals changed with the arrival and departure of managers, staff and children, not to mention with new priorities and approaches. Only the *Children Act,* 1989 remained the same, continuing in splendid isolation from much that was happening in the residential setting.

As can be seen in Chapter Six, these categories of structures can be analysed and illustrated diagrammatically. Moreover, the research has identified a set of questions which managers can ask of their own home to see how they are performing.

## Studying the culture of homes

Similar research techniques helped to clarify the cultural aspects of homes. Building on Gouldner's work, homes were studied to see if the staff and/or children responded as a group to a set of problems and tasks common in residential care. If they did, further analysis was undertaken to see whether or not there was cohesion within the staff or child group. This scrutiny focused on tasks within each of the six dimensions of a child's life used in successive Dartington studies, that is; the child's living situation; family and social relationships; social and anti-social behaviour; physical and psychological health; education and employment; and dependency on services. The tasks within each dimension were linked to the goals - societal, formal and belief - of the home as previously discussed. So, under living situations, one question asked of staff was 'what do you do when a new child arrives in this unit?', a question which was also asked of children to explore the child culture of the home. Answers were assessed in conjunction with other information, such as the observations of the researchers on such events. For education and employment, a question explored how staff and children reacted to a child refusing to go to school, and so on. The list of questions that proved most useful is in Appendix Three and has been used to frame the practice discussion in Chapter 10.

This approach bore fruit. First, it established whether there was a culture within the home and, where it existed, explored its nature. For example, in some homes there were several sub-cultures, while in others the group response of staff and children was nothing more than unthinking habit. Second, it was possible to gauge whether the culture was concordant with the various goals of the residential centre, that is to provide an effective Part III child care service, to achieve the stated aims and objectives of the institution and to fulfil the beliefs of the manager. Third, because the ideas informing the study were manifest empirically, that is boiled down to questions to which any manager could find answers, there was a prospect of finding remedies to common problems in children's homes.

All of this would only be of limited academic interest if it did not help managers understand practice. As will be shown, the ideas explain how children's homes change over time, why some homes are better than others and why some do well with seemingly unpromising residents. The analysis revealed some clear patterns, as the following pages illustrate.

## Predicting change in children's homes

It will be seen in Chapter Five that there was considerable change over the year in the nine homes scrutinised. Some of this change could be described as development, some instability. The key to explaining why good homes suddenly deteriorated or bad homes experienced a spell of tranquillity lay somewhere in the relationship between structure, staff culture and child culture. The starting point had to be the structural aspects of homes - the societal, formal and belief goals as defined above.

In homes where there was concordance between the formal goals (that is what the home was trying to achieve, for which groups of children and by what method), the beliefs of the manager and the societal goals (as manifest in the *Children Act*, 1989 and Volume Four of the associated Guidance), the staff culture tended to complement the home's aims and objectives. Where there was discord between the different types of goals, staff cultures were either so weak as to be virtually absent or cohered to undermine all that the manager wished to achieve.

In Chapter Six it is seen that in Blue home the manager barely knew of the existence of the Guidance and was extremely hazy about the principles underpinning the legislation. He believed passionately in the children sheltered but expectations tended to be unrealistic, for example, thinking that young people could be returned to mainstream schools without additional support or that long-standing family problems could be alleviated by counselling from untrained residential workers. When the staff culture was measured (by asking questions about their response to common tasks in the home), little in the way of coherence emerged. In some areas, for instance, how to restrain a child, there was common agreement but on other issues such as how to greet a visiting parent, whether children should do homework or what to do if a resident stayed out late, staff produced an array of contradictory responses. Lack of concordance between the structural dimensions of the home resulted in a fragmented staff culture.

The absence of any apparent group response at one moment in time could not be taken as evidence of continual division between staff. In some homes, culture could be considered as latent, emerging in response to specific issues, such as sexual activity between residents or the breakdown of the omnipresent 'rota' that sets out who works which shift. The nature of these latent cultures could be instructive. Clearly, there is a difference between a staff group rising up in indignation because a leaver failed to get appropriate after care services and a row over 'split shifts' and who should work on a Wednesday afternoon. Both are important but only the former is instrumental to the societal and formal goals of homes.

The strength of the staff culture and its concordance with the structural goals of the home were found to influence the likelihood of a child culture emerging. In *Issues of Control in Residential Care*, it is stated that good homes 'make efforts to fragment the informal world of children by a variety of structural features, for example by appointing senior children to positions of responsibility'. What was surprising about this study was the infrequency with which coherent child cultures emerged; there was seldom much for staff to fragment. Nonetheless, in Cyan, where the staff culture reflected the overarching goal to provide a safe environment in which residents' problems could be addressed, children's responses to difficult situations were entirely appropriate. So, a child who ran away would explain his or her misbehaviour to the 'group' comprising both staff and residents, with the children asking questions that were just as searching as those posed by the staff. Staff culture and child culture were thus concordant.

This vista of ordered life in a well organised residential centre is unfortunately not universal. In some of the centres visited, the picture was very different. Where homes had no clear structure or where elements of the structure conflicted and where staff responses to tasks were incoherent, it was possible for a child culture to emerge which was counter to the best interests of residents. At Indigo, for example, as will be illustrated in later chapters, a child culture of non-school attendance, drug misuse and petty crime flared up in response to an inadequate structure and discordant staff group responses. But sub-cultures, such as those identified in studies of larger institutions like mental hospitals, prisons and public schools, are rare in the smaller children's homes and, where they do exist, are frequently transitory.

The final part of the analysis was to discover whether homes with concordant societal, formal and belief goals, a staff culture which was in harmony with the structure, and a child culture which was either fragmented or congruent with the aims and objectives of the residential centre were better than those where the opposite patterns prevailed. It should not spoil the suspense to report here that this hypothesis was proven in the sense that the better homes, as measured on independent outcome measures, displayed similar patterns in the relationship between the factors described. Much of the study is devoted to explaining how these results were found and how all children's homes can emulate the best.

## Outcomes

To reach this point, it had to be possible to identify a good home. Outcomes were measured in several ways. On first encounter, each researcher applied the principles underpinning the *Children Act,* 1989 and the recommendations of the Guidance to see how far these seemed to be implemented. These assessments should not be dismissed since many professionals seeking placements for children base their judgements on observations made during visits. Thereafter, key aspects of the homes were noted, such as whether the place was flexible to children's changing needs, did the children want to live there and were adequate arrangements for young people's future made on leaving? This analysis was aided by the concurrent work of Sinclair and Gibbs on *Quality of Care in Children's Homes* and the results presented in Chapter Eight include some of the outcome variables used in their study.

None of this would have mattered if the good homes did not achieve positive outcomes for the children involved. As described in the next chapter, the study monitored the progress of all children in the nine homes at the beginning of the study, including just over a quarter of them in considerable depth. It is heartening to report that, generally speaking, there is a positive link between the performance of the home, as assessed on the dimensions just described, and the adaptations of children within those homes.

If this analysis holds up - and the reader must be the judge of this - it offers the prospect of a direct link between the structure of children's homes, the culture within their walls, the quality of the residential experience and the outcomes for children placed therein. By understanding these relationships and having practice tools to explore them, managers should be in a better position to improve the quality of residential care and promote the welfare of children.

## Conclusion

The focus of this study is children's homes and the purpose is to explore the links between structure, staff and child cultures and outcomes. Most treatises on residential care emphasise the importance of staff and residents' cultures as a variable affecting institutional performance but the precise relationship has remained unclear, especially for establishments less rumbustious than those most frequently studied, such as large mental hospitals or prisons. The connection is equally important for community homes but is more difficult to study. Cultures, if they exist, are unlikely to display the rigidity and brutal enforcement of total institutions and practice is much more legally directed. Nevertheless, they are highly likely to influence children's responses and behaviour and cannot be ignored just because they are more difficult to assess on predetermined criteria.

The contribution of this study is to chart and analyse the staff and child cultures that exist in children's homes in the mid 1990s. Thus, past assumptions will be re-examined. Additionally, the interaction between staff and child cultures will be explored along with the factors, especially organisational structures, that affect them. Whatever relationships are found will be related to outcomes for homes and for children.

This exercise has three benefits. It goes beyond the tautological conclusion that a good home is one where staff know what they are doing because they work in a good home. It does this by linking features of structure and culture to independently measured outcomes, evaluated on *Children Act* principles. Secondly, a perspective that views the whole institution and charts change over time will avoid the tendency to draw crude conclusions from statistical correlation. It has been noted, for example, that the proportion of trained staff in homes does not correlate with homes ranked in order of good outcomes, suggesting for some that training does not matter. To view training as promoting new ideas and confidence applied in the context of a changing structure and culture not only helps explain the weak statistical association but also offers ways of improving the situation.

Finally, it is clear that an academic project such as this is of little use on its own. It is equally the case that single and simple interventions have not improved the quality of residential care. If analytic tools can be developed from the research to help managers better diagnose the complexity of residential establishments they are more likely to arrive at solutions. Thus, research and practice will be more closely linked and the problems of poor management, identified in so many inquiry reports, will begin to be addressed.

# 3 How the research was done

It can be seen from what has just been written that the study demanded a variety of information from several sources. The ideas put forward at the outset required that part of the study should be about the structure of children's homes - their goals and objectives; partly about the culture of these places, particularly the way staff and children responded to the home's goals; and partly about outcomes, both for the homes themselves and the children living in them. Moreover, it was necessary to see if any relationship could be found between data collected in each of these areas which itself implied a requirement that information be summarised in such a way that it could be compared, cross-tabulated and checked.

The initial task was to identify some residential centres suitable for the study. It might have been appropriate to invest all the research energy into understanding one home; many investigations have profitably done just this. But there are dangers in single institution studies. Were all mental hospitals like that described by Goffman? In previous Dartington studies of approved schools, secure units, prisons and children's homes, a variety of institutional aims, structures and staff and inmate cultures, ranging from 'total institutions' to 'therapeutic communities' had been found within one sector of residential care. So a single case study was quickly discarded as an option for the purposes of this investigation.

But how many homes would be needed to get a representative picture? A review of the available statistics and research evidence clarified the number and characteristics of children in different types of residence and established how long they stayed, why they were there and what sort of service they received. The results of this work have been reported in *A Life Without Problems*. It was concluded that nine homes would be needed to cover differences of legal status, size, location and function and to permit an intensive look at each one. Ideally, an additional look at a secure unit would have been undertaken, as this sector poses very different questions on the structure and culture of residence, but this was beyond the scope of the investigation. The actual homes selected are described in the following chapter.

Having chosen the homes, the primary task became finding methods that would enable the study to show how the structures and cultures of homes combine to produce beneficial outcomes.

## Understanding structure

The homes had to be visited. The duration and timing of these visits posed a dilemma. A day would not be sufficient but several weeks would be too much; not to say a less than propitious use of research resources. One long visit was also thought unsatisfactory. Most residential establishments go through bad patches when children run away, cause concern in the local community or simply fail to get along with one another. Staff too can lurch from buoyant confidence to despair and cynicism. Understanding these cycles of changes was central to our aim of getting an accurate picture of life within residence. Several visits over time were therefore necessary.

Each home was studied over a period of one calendar year. After an initial preparatory visit, the fieldwork took place over three days and nights. This was repeated a year later. In between, day visits were made every six weeks and between these there were regular telephone calls and letters to and from staff and children.

At the outset, all of the written material about the home was collected. This gave an indication of the formal goals for each residential centre. Most had what is termed a 'statement of purpose and function' which roughly means 'what the home is meant to do each day for children in need'. Sometimes there would be other papers for staff, children or their families. Judgements had to be made. A home which states it caters for eight to 11 year olds might, in fact, be sheltering adolescents, and proud claims to be acting on the principles of the *Children Act*, 1989 count for little if the manager has not understood the legislation and staff are not familiar with the associated guidance.

To understand the formal goals of the home, that is what it sought to do under the conditions in which it operated and the children being referred for help, more detailed information was required. The home's statement of purpose and function was the main source of information on these formal goals, but a 'homes overview' questionnaire was also completed. Data were drawn from several sources, including managers, professionals, children and families inside and outside of the residential centre. Again, there were occasionally contradictions in what was being said to the researchers and judgements had to be made about what was actually happening. The same questions about the formal dimensions of the home were asked again a year later, thus enabling the development of a picture of change in the nine homes.

So much for what the home was doing; what did the manager believe about practice in his or her residential centre? In essence this was established through in-depth interviews at the beginning and end of the fieldwork or the manager's tenure (each manager of the home was interviewed at least twice). These discussions were sufficiently detailed for it to be possible to make a distinction between what a manager believed and what he or she said they believed. Clearly somebody who expresses an unerring commitment to a particular home but is also known to be applying for posts elsewhere has conflicting interests and it was necessary to make some form of decision about where loyalties lay.

Through these mechanisms it was possible, over time, to build up a picture of the societal, formal and belief goals of the nine homes and the relationship between these dimensions. The bulk of the work was undertaken by the two researchers but for every home an independent observer with a research background joined them both for the fieldwork and data analysis. Thus, it was possible to be reasonably confident about the quality of judgements being made.

None of the above would have much meaning without being sure of the quality of practice within the nine homes and the circumstances of the children residing there. When the manager talked of the needs of the child, how did this compare with the characteristics of the residents? When the statement of purpose and function sets out the therapeutic strengths of the placement, where was the evidence of staff qualified to fulfil these claims? Data on children and staff were, therefore, a pre-requisite.

A start was made by collecting information on all children resident on the first day of the study. Their files were the first port of call.

Frequently, these were sparse or had sections left incomplete; a finding in its own right. This led to interviews with residential social workers, field workers and, where possible, the children themselves, until sufficient data was obtained. This process was repeated at the end of the fieldwork period, 12 months later.

Gathering facts about the staff was more difficult. There is less recorded about them in files. There are, generally, more of them than children. All senior staff were interviewed at least three times during the course of the study and others at least once. In addition, all staff were invited to complete an extensive questionnaire. This was only partially successful in that while the response rate was 100% in two homes, it was less than 50% in four. To reinforce information collected in this way, two staff in each home were selected as case studies and regularly interviewed in depth. Overall, enough data were assembled to provide a satisfactory picture of the situation of residential social workers and other staff in the nine homes.

## Understanding cultures

Gathering factual information on the staff and children in homes is relatively straightforward compared with the task of understanding cultures within these residential centres; this requires an analysis over and above the individuals within residence. Culture, in the way it is defined in the previous chapter, may persist despite people's comings and goings and new arrivals, whether staff or children, will be socialised into the home's way of life. Conversely, staff or residents may bring a culture into a home so that the charismatic, the zealot, the thug or the tearaway can set the tone of institutional life and generate responses among others working or living in the home.

The primary method for understanding the culture was what Hammersley and Atkinson call 'non-participant observation'; meaning that the researcher joins in the life of the place he or she is researching, observes what is going on but remains a researcher (that is to say, does not attempt to obscure his or her role or take on the tasks of those being studied). This is not to say that the researchers do not take proper care in placing children and staff at ease, giving them the opportunity to forget that they are under scrutiny.

The three day visits at the beginning and end of the study, taken together with the intermittent contacts in between, gave ample opportunity to observe the culture of the homes. Whenever possible, all parts of the daily routine, from breakfast to bedtime, were monitored. This often involved researchers staying overnight.

As with most qualitative research, the difficulty swiftly became how to organise and analyse the amount of information being collected. Early on, it was decided to concentrate on tasks within the homes, looking at how staff and children responded and whether or not they responded in the same way. For example, the researchers watched what happened when a family member visited the home. Naturally, it was important to know if staff behaved sensitively and whether children were prepared. But for the purposes of this study, the primary concern was to see if staff and then children reacted in a similar fashion to each other. Evidence of co-incidence of actions and views was an indicator that a culture existed among staff or children.

In this respect, the behaviour of staff was a good deal easier to monitor than that of the children. More sensitive techniques were required to get some insight into what the residents felt about different aspects of life in the home or the reasons why they responded as they did to different tasks. The children were interviewed on each visit, either individually or in groups, about the tasks the home was intended to perform. Responses varied by home and time of visit but every child was involved in some way. Those children selected as case studies were encouraged to keep diaries, a method used to great effect in several studies of residential care. Children in each of the residential centres were also offered the use of a video camera to make a film of life in the home.

## Understanding outcome

This is not the place for a long treatise on the concept of outcome. Suffice to say that much has been written on this issue and the seminal text remains Parker and colleagues' *Looking After Children: Assessing Outcomes in Child Care*. The methodological questions for this study were how to understand outcomes of a home and how to relate this to information collected on outcomes for the children sheltered within these homes. Finding answers largely centred on finding the right distinction between process outcomes - roughly speaking what professionals do to help the child - and real outcomes - what actually

happens to the child; does he or she prosper or suffer by
in residential care?

Data were collected on three aspects of life within th
factors such as whether an individual care plan was set o
or the numbers running away were high; perceptions of t...... ...... ....
working in the home, particularly did they think it was a good place to
be and could they see a good reason for being there; and the researchers'
rating of whether the home as structured was capable of achieving the
aims and objectives it set for itself. This information was accrued from
the same sources described above.

Understanding outcomes for the children was relatively
straightforward since it was possible to fall back on methods used in
recent Dartington studies, for example, of leavers from specialised
secure treatment centres. Initially, for each child resident at the
beginning of the study, information recorded in the file was used to set
out, from a research perspective, what was likely to be achieved if the
care plan - where there was one - was fully implemented. This
projected outcome was then compared with the child's progress over
the following 12 months. Second, the last two entrants in each home
were selected for intensive follow-up. Here, a more detailed prognosis
was drawn up and, where information was missing from the care plan,
it was sought from other sources. The children and, where possible,
their family members were interviewed. Third, the *Looking After
Children* instruments - derived from the Parker and colleagues' study
mentioned above and which allow for a systematic monitoring of
outcomes in all areas of a child's life - were applied at the beginning
and end of the fieldwork to the same children involved in the intensive
follow-up. This was a collaborative process between the child and his or
her 'key worker' except in two cases where, for a variety of reasons, the
forms had to be completed by the researchers asking the questions of
the key workers.

## Bringing together the data on structure, culture and outcomes

The result of all this endeavour was a wealth of data from several
sources. None of the information had been collected unnecessarily. It
all had a purpose. The difficulty was to link what had been learned
about the children's homes so as to produce findings sufficiently robust

to satisfy independent scientific scrutiny but also be relevant to policy makers and practitioners operating in this area.

The combination of methods produced, as had been hoped, information on:

- the structure of the homes
- the staff culture of the homes
- the child culture of the homes
- the outcome for the homes, and
- the outcome for children living in the homes.

Some associations between these dimensions were manifest to the researchers involved in the fieldwork but, to test them carefully, it was necessary to produce summary variables which captured the essence of what had been discovered. So, the formal goals of the home - one part of the structure - were reduced to a small number of questions about what needs were being met, whether the staff had skills to meet those needs and whether the building was appropriate for the children accommodated. The service factors in residence - one aspect of outcomes of homes - were also reduced to a few proxy questions about aims and objectives, the accessibility of information and the presence of individual care plans.

This work, undertaken in the safe haven of a research unit, was successful in as much as a clear relationship between structure, cultures and outcomes was uncovered. But there was a danger that cold analysis would have little meaning back in the hothouse of residence. So the results were tested again, concentrating as much on why some factors seemed unimportant in explaining an outcome as on why others were important. At the same time, the results were re-analysed using techniques appropriate for small scale statistics.

## Conclusion: producing a practice tool

The method of working described in this chapter raises two important issues. The first concerns the link between theory and method, a relationship explored in Brannen's book on *Mixing Methods*. It is argued that it is helpful if middle range theory from one set of research is used to structure a new study. Much data, quantitative and qualitative, are collected from several sources; probably more than can be used in the final explanation but sufficient to ensure that the subject of study is fully understood. This is then reduced to proxy variables that explain the relationship between the principal dimensions of the study; in the case of this research, structure, culture and outcome. The final model is then taken back to the data source and tested again, both quantitatively and qualitatively.

A second issue concerns the relationship between research and development. It is hoped that this and other research will lead to the development of a practice tool that allows managers to take a look at their home, examine its formal and informal worlds, and so identify weaknesses (and therefore suggest remedies) in the way it is run. Once there is general satisfaction with the validity of the product, it will be made available for general distribution.

This approach may seem strange to a psychologist used to validating tools prior to the fieldwork getting underway, ideally uncontaminated by the rigours of practice. Neither would the design appeal to the orthodox qualitative researcher used to collecting large amounts of information without worrying too much about the relationships within the data set or what is being explained. Somewhere between these two there seems to be an approach that does not offend the scientist, anxious to know that the results stand up to independent testing, or the professional charged with meeting the needs of vulnerable children. It is this middle path that this study takes.

# 4 The homes described

Nine homes were selected to provide a representative sample of residential care for children looked after in England and Wales. This chapter describes them as they appeared to the researchers at the beginning of the study. Initially, selected data on residential care for looked after children are provided to allow readers to judge how the nine homes in the study compare. Then, information on the characteristics of children and staff is offered. The substantive part of the chapter, however, is given to a description of each home, showing similarities and unique characteristics which can be used to compare their development as it unfolds in subsequent chapters.

## Residential care for children looked after

Department of Health statistics show that in 1996 there were 1,200 children's homes in England. Two thirds were provided by local authorities, the remainder being run either by voluntary or private organisations. As mentioned at the outset, the number of residents has been falling for some time: in 1996 in England just 6,820 children were looked after. The proportion of beds provided by the private sector meanwhile continues to increase. The following table summarises the general picture.

Table 4.1: Children looked after in children's homes in England at 31st March 1993, 1994, 1995 and 1996 by provider of placement

| Year | Provider of Home | | | |
| | Local authority | Voluntary | Private | Total |
|------|-----------------|-----------|---------|-------|
| 1993 | 7,700 | 810 | 440 | 8,950 |
| 1994 | 6,500 | 820 | 680 | 8,000 |
| 1995 | 5,700 | 567 | 648 | 6,915 |
| 1996 | 5,500 | 490 | 830 | 6,820 |

Of the nine homes eventually selected for this study, six were provided by four different local authorities, two by voluntary agencies and one was privately run.

In *Children in the Public Care*, Utting recommended that children's homes should have a minimum of 4 and a maximum of 14 beds. Most commonly, local authority homes have six or fewer places although Warner's survey found a considerable range in size, with homes in the voluntary sector offering 16 beds on average. As will be seen, the homes selected for this study had between 5 and 12 places, although one in the voluntary sector and the private home were part of larger residential campuses looking after up to 80 children.

As the findings presented in Chapter Two revealed, many children placed in residential care stay a comparatively short time. The nine homes selected offered placements of different lengths; one offered respite care, two enabled children to stay up to six months (in fact most stayed much less than this) and six were long term. Thus, children's average length of stay was slightly longer than might have been expected from national figures but the range was very wide indeed.

Both Wagner and Utting considered that residential care would continue to be the best option to meet certain needs of children - respite care, preparation for permanent placements, keeping sibling groups together, therapeutic provision for socially and emotionally damaged children and, lastly, care and control in secure accommodation. Within reasonable limits, the nine homes selected attempted to meet one or more of these needs, with the exception of secure accommodation which, as has been mentioned, was excluded from the study. In addition, it was possible to achieve geographical spread for the research, with five of the homes sited in cities and the others in rural areas.

## Characteristics of the children in the nine homes

Warner found the average age of children looked after in residential care to be 14 years; local authority statistical returns show increasing proportions of older teenagers and Utting concluded that residential care is now a service mainly for adolescents. Nevertheless, there are younger children in residence, with at least 15% under 10 years old. The nine homes in this study reflected this pattern. Of the 65 children resident on the first day of fieldwork, 17% were under 10, 77% were aged 10 to 15 and 6% were 16 or over. Comparison between the characteristics of the children and national figures provided by Department of Health, The Social Services Inspectorate and the University of York indicates that the young people accommodated at the first visit for this study were similar in terms of gender but were a little bit younger and stayed slightly longer.

Traditionally, residential care has been used more for boys than girls and 40 of the 65 children in the nine homes were male. All but one of the nine homes cared for girls and boys, the exception admitting only girls. This pattern reflects that which exists nationally, whereby nine out of ten children looked after in residential homes live in coeducational settings.

In selecting homes, the ethnic background of residents was considered. In *Child Care Now*, Rowe and colleagues found children of mixed parentage to be over represented in residence with those from Asian families slightly under represented. Success in replicating this pattern was only partial. Of the 65 children studied, less than a quarter (23%) came from a minority ethnic group and most of those lived in one of the nine homes. (Of the 65 children, 8% were of mixed parentage, 9% Afro Caribbean and 6% Asian).

In terms of legal status and background characteristics, the young people varied considerably, making it difficult to define 'a typical' resident or specify a single reason for their being admitted to the homes. For example, while the majority (58%) were accommodated voluntarily, 3% were on remand and 38% on court orders. Nearly a third (29%) of admissions were emergencies, 69% had experienced a placement breakdown and 10% had been looked after for more than half their life. The range of presenting problems was equally wide but no single factor was sufficiently common to dominate the resident population. For instance 14% had a history of offending and 34%, 44% and 25% were known to be victims of physical, sexual and emotional abuse respectively. The main reasons for admission to the homes were being beyond control (58%), abuse (18%), offending (8%), respite (8%) and family breakdown (6%). However, many children were multiply disadvantaged and the incidence of these difficulties was not only higher but the severity was also exacerbated by failure, rejection and poor self esteem. Despite the variety of situations, the combination of trauma, deprivation and antisocial behaviour was apparent from the figures obtained.

## Characteristics of staff in the nine homes

Warner estimated that in 1992 there were 15,000 care staff working in children's residential homes. The survey for the Inquiry found staff had a mean age of 35 with officers in charge five years older. Just a third of those running homes and only seven per cent of those they managed had a professional social work qualification. Usually, staff stayed in post for three years, although those in both the private and voluntary sectors stayed for shorter periods of time. Sickness levels were lowest in the private home. Vacancy rates and the use of agency staff were highest in local authority homes.

At the outset, 123 care staff (i.e. excluding the manager, domestic and administrative staff) were employed in the nine homes. Sixteen of these, in four of the homes, worked part time. The characteristics of these staff varied considerably. Some teams were stable, comprising workers in post for over 10 years; some teams were predominately women and some had high numbers of part time and temporary staff. The average age of staff was similar to Warner's 35 years, but this disguised two staff groups in their 20's and two others where the mean age was 45 years. Only five per cent of care staff and four of the nine officers in charge had social work qualifications. Two-fifths were men. Full details of this evidence on children and staff in the homes can be found in Appendix Two.

The characteristics of the homes studied are summarised in the following table. They are compared on nine dimensions comprising plant, location and the background characteristics of children and staff. In some aspects, such as the number of qualified staff, they are all fairly similar, but in others, such as children's length of stay, there is considerable variation.

The homes are not a perfect fit with the national scene but the picture is broadly right and, certainly, the addition of more places would have been counter-productive to the study's aims and objectives.

Table 4.2: The characteristics of the nine homes selected for study

The Nine Homes

| Characteristics | B | Y | G | R | M | O | C | I | W |
|---|---|---|---|---|---|---|---|---|---|
| Provider | LA | Vol | LA | LA | Private | LA | Vol | LA | LA |
| Location | City | Rural | City | City | Rural | City | Rural | Town | City |
| Number of beds | 11 | 5 | 12 | 6 | 6 | 6 | 9 | 10 | 8 |
| Age range | 13+ | 0-19 | 11-17 | 16+ | 12+ | 0-13 | 9-15 | 13-16 | 11-16 |
| Gender of child | Both | Both | Both | Both | Girls | Both | Both | Both | Both |
| Length of stay | Med* | Resp* | Med | Med* | Long | Long | Long | Med* | Med |
| Number of staff# | 16 | 14 | 22 | 12 | 9 | 17 | 9 | 16 | 8 |
| Qual' manager | No | Yes | Yes | No | No | Yes | No | Yes | No |
| Qualified staff | 2 | 0 | 0 | 0 | 0 | 2 | 1 | 1 | 0 |

* = emergency admissions also possible
# = excluding the manager, domestic and administrative staff

## First impressions of the nine homes

One of the aims of the study is to provide managers with ways of understanding the functioning of the homes for which they are responsible. As professionals implementing the *Children Act*, 1989, what would they have seen on the first day they entered any one of the nine homes selected for scrutiny? The first impressions of the researchers are recorded here. There is no logical way of ordering these descriptions so, for clarity, they are divided into three groups: small local authority homes (up to eight children); medium sized local authority run homes; and homes run by voluntary or private agencies.

### Small local authority homes

*Orange*

Orange was established in 1984 as a therapeutic unit for six children aged under 13. The home had previously been one unit in a large observation and assessment centre serving a city of 350,000 and its rural environs. Having no need for 'O & A', the building was adapted to provide four children's homes, each with different aims and objectives. All four have to make what they can of the site situated in a city park within a middle class neighbourhood.

The old O & A centre had been split four ways and inside Orange further divisions appeared. To the left of the front door was child space and to the right the staff area. The left was full of colour and noise of children competing for attention and toys; the right was organised into neatly segregated offices in which staff stayed unless called to duty. These offices were out of bounds to the children.

Seventeen permanent staff worked here, but a glance at the rota revealed high sickness levels and unfilled vacancies. Relief staff were regularly used, making communication and consistency of approach a problem. Two of the 17 staff were qualified social workers and a small core had many years of residential experience. But others were actively and vociferously seeking to get out and the general impression was of a tired and dispirited band, unsure of their task with the children. The basic rules were to avoid confrontations and stay in the office. As one senior staff member was heard to say to a demanding child, 'We're not here for your benefit you know'.

If the staff were ambivalent about the children, then it is unsurprising to discover that the children were ambivalent about the staff. To get into Orange, they had to be long separated and difficult to place. Noisy, boisterous and attention seeking, the children all knew that Orange was a bridge, albeit a long bridge, to another substitute family placement. Some had occasional visits from relatives. All considered field social workers as the principal decision makers in their lives. The children appeared to have little love for one another. They rarely played group games or displayed much mutual interest. On rare occasions the group did coalesce; for example when they went to the pantomime or, more frequently, when the group huddled together whilst one of the group was controlled by staff. Sitting between the staff and children was an education specialist who supported the children's school placements. She was a hive of activity, buzzing between schools, smoothing over problems and helping children with their considerable special education needs. The saving grace of the placement, therefore, was that all the children went to school.

So much for therapy. Only the bike shed brought staff and children together. Here staff congregated to smoke. The children were too young to smoke but staff turned a blind eye and many happy conversations between adults and residents took place in this unprepossessing location. Once back inside the home, divisions re-emerged and communication withered. This appeared, at first sight, to be a home divided and lacking in belief.

*Red*

The second small local authority home was called Red. Part of a city council estate, there was little to distinguish this terrace of three houses from its immediate neighbours. The front door was regularly open, allowing adolescents in jeans and sweatshirts to wander in and out. Inside a slightly shabby, poorly lit and colourless interior was brightened by the chatter of young people and staff, sitting in the lounge together drinking coffee from chipped mugs.

Red housed six young people aged 16 and over in a series of bedsits. They were being prepared for independent living, an experience intended to last between six and 12 months. The downstairs space belonged to everyone; the offices were unlocked and everyone had access to the phones. Local young people and neighbours popped in and out, chipping into the conversations about court appearances, jobs and behaviour at will.

The young people nevertheless posed plenty of problems for staff. Some were delinquent, some had been abused and others could be described as disturbed. All had been tried and had failed in other placements. At the time, all were boys, but girls and girlfriends were often at the house, creating potential control problems. Ex-residents also regularly called in for coffee, a chat and some company. Fights, drugs and theft were not unknown but staff and children were clear that such behaviours were not acceptable within the home.

The task of keeping order fell to 12 staff, six men and six women, who spent much of their time helping the young people to get work experience, understand social security benefits, find places to live and putting in a good word for them in court. None had formal qualifications but their interests and practical skills which included motor mechanics, orienteering, climbing, knitting, cooking and others besides, were displayed on the office wall. They worked with determination, humour and energy and, in the sense that residents liked the place and wanted to stay, with a measure of success.

Just as the fieldwork began, the manager who had established this seemingly disorganised but effective regime was promoted to another post. Two assistant managers took her place, although never a week went by without the previous incumbent calling in. The potential for change in this apparently effective unit seemed considerable at the start of the study.

## White

The third small local authority home, White, also catered for adolescents. It would be difficult to know from the outside that this large semi-detached Victorian villa by the sea sheltered eight young people. The decor and furnishings downstairs had been chosen by past residents and reflected the child centred nature of the regime here. In the sitting room the children niggled at each other for possession of the most comfortable chair; in the games room, bean bags and chairs were pulled up around computers. White's aim was to provide a home until the young people could move on to a more permanent placement; a 'holding facility' to use the nomenclature. Needless to say, many residents stayed beyond the intended maximum of six months.

Only eight staff, none of whom was qualified, were employed here. To ensure that the young people were cared for, teams of two worked 24 hour shifts. Three of the team had worked together for 20 years and each seemed to have confidence in their colleagues' methods, routines and practice. Their talk was about young people's stability, warmth and understanding. They had no special approach and no particular plans other than to run a peaceful, uncontentious home.

White's residents all came from the locality and continued to attend their original schools. Four of the seven were away from home for the first time. All were considered 'beyond parental control' but none had a history of delinquency and only one was known to have been abused. It was difficult to know why residential care had been preferred to foster care for these children and, as a group, they acted as a large family might be expected to behave.

In the year prior to the research team's involvement, the manager who had been there for a quarter of a century retired. She had believed that the mission of the home was to give food and shelter to children and her long-stay, largely female staff team embraced this philosophy wholeheartedly. The new manager had certificates for residential work and some previous experience, though he lacked a recognised social work qualification. He complained that young people were 'dumped' far too easily by their families onto local authorities who left the front doors of their children's homes open too readily. The White staff team accepted his views quiescently since he changed little about the way they had been working for so long.

## Larger local authority homes

*Blue*

Three of the homes included in the study were slightly larger, offering nine or more beds. The first of these, Blue, managed to maintain a family-like feel to it. Eleven children from a variety of ethnic backgrounds lived here, cared for by 16 similarly diverse staff. Run by an outer London borough, Blue was situated on an island of grass in the midst of a low rise council estate; only the presence of a dozen milk bottles outside each door suggested that more than the average sized family lived in the two houses knocked together to preserve the anonymity of the home. Inside, there were two TV rooms, two staircases, two bathrooms, the two halves of the building joined by one ground floor kitchen. At the beginning of the study, Blue primarily cared for younger children, including groups of siblings, awaiting long term fostering or adoption. As will be seen, the aims and objectives of the home changed completely during the study period.

All but 4 of the 16 staff were women and 12 were of Afro-Caribbean origin. Most were mothers themselves. It was hard to tell whether the beliefs and values they shared reflected cultural roots, overlapping life experiences, or simply a long professional association and a democratic style of decision making. Whatever the cause, the effect was a stable staff group who shared the same ideas of what they were doing and why.

*Indigo*

Indigo, the second of the larger local authority homes had 10 beds only 6 of which were occupied at the beginning of the fieldwork. An adolescent boy, Gary, initially accepted as an emergency overnight placement, had six months later brought the home to a standstill with his violent and mercurial behaviour. This was evident on the researchers' first visit, as Gary ruined a mealtime by rushing from person to person, plate to plate, teasing and antagonising the children and forcing first the clerical and domestic staff then the care staff and researchers to take refuge in the office away from the rampaging outside. Having initiated the researchers, staff began to talk about what is was really like in the home and throughout the following year, a sad picture of an institution in crisis emerged.

Indigo was designed to offer short, medium and long term care for boys and girls aged 13 to 16. It was meant to be flexible, undertaking assessment, supporting placements and families, offering crisis intervention, preparing children for new placements and providing family therapy. The paperwork suggested that Indigo met every conceivable need: in reality it found it difficult to meet any. Located in a rural town, Indigo sat between a comprehensive school and a police station. Unfortunately, none of the children attended school, requiring staff to mind the children during the day, so leaving little or no time for paperwork, training or supervision. The police station was more useful as a resource for refereeing fights and restraining the recalcitrant; indeed, entertaining residents was routine.

The staff consistently complained that they were being sent the wrong children. Five boys and one pregnant girl were resident at the beginning of the fieldwork. Like the staff, residents had little sense of what they were doing in the home or the purpose of their stay. Nor did they believe that Indigo could achieve something positive for them. They wandered around the house and town, grasping attention wherever they could. A number of incidents where children needed to be restrained occurred outside the locked office door, wherein staff sheltered. The young people used children's meetings to change routines and rules to suit. One was a regular drug user and running away was frequent.

Again, on paper, the odds seemed to favour the staff. They outnumbered children by two to one. They appeared a talented and experienced team. Two were qualified social workers, another seven had relevant training and the others had considerable residential child care experience. But they were fragmented and lacked direction, purpose and belief. They doggedly coped with restraint after restraint, struggling to keep a sense of humour. 'Working at Indigo', said one carer, 'is abusive to staff and children'.

*Green*

The last medium sized local authority home was Green. Conveniently situated in the suburbs of a busy, cosmopolitan city, Green was home for 12 young people aged 11 to 17, for up to six months. At first sight, the home seemed to be decorated and furnished to appeal more to the elderly than to adolescents. There were no signs of any toys or games and the few books rarely left the shelves. Upstairs, posters and photographs were on display in the bedrooms but the house still felt more like a boarding school than a home.

Children were admitted for a wide range of problems and six were victims of sexual abuse. The home sought to help residents understand why they were separated from their families, to improve their self image and attend to their educational needs. Not unnaturally, some of the young people found trusting adults and peers difficult and the child group was rarely cohesive. Abusive language, aggression and attention seeking behaviour were not unusual. Nevertheless, an order and routine were imposed. Most children went to school and those excluded, temporarily or permanently, were expected to dress in school uniform and do work sent by the school, supervised by a member of staff.

Fourteen of the 22 staff were men. Only the manager was qualified. The staff worked in three distinct teams, each with a different idea of their role. One group believed they had a responsibility to make the children's stay as pleasant as possible. Another felt they 'shouldn't entertain the children too much or they wouldn't want to go home', while the third was satisfied with routine supervision to prevent violent and abusive incidents. It was difficult for the researchers to get a sense of this home as each time the shifts changed, so did the focus of the work.

Although the six homes just described were run by local authorities, each functioned in diverse ways. Some staff groups appeared much more confident and focused than others, yet their performance seemed unrelated to experience, level of training or the ratio of staff to children. Some groups of residents, such as the young people at Red, worked together with the staff towards the same goals. Others had little idea of what their placements were supposed to achieve and actively undermined staff attempts to help. In all cases, the facts on paper about size, remit, staff and children were of little help in preparing the visitor for what existed in practice.

### Private and voluntary homes

#### Magenta

The final three homes were provided by the voluntary and private sectors. The private home, Magenta, offered long term care and education for 45 adolescent girls. The study focused upon Central House of Magenta which accommodated six girls. Magenta was created by a social worker and a teacher, both entrepreneurs, who acted as directors of the business. The two social workers managing Magenta were the only qualified staff of the 40 on site. Magenta set out to provide the girls with what was described as a model of responsible parenting, such as how to run a house, keep medical appointments and bring up children. The directors believed all young women could benefit from this approach and few referrals were ever refused a place.

Magenta was situated in converted farm buildings in a rural county. Central House was the largest on campus, the other residents lived in groups of three in rented houses nearby. All the houses were expensively decorated in a Laura Ashley style of old pine and chintz. In the bathrooms, bottles of lotions, gels and perfumes filled the shelves; attention to appearance was encouraged. Nonetheless, the swimming pool and volley ball nets struggled to compete with the patio, the designated place for sharing a cigarette. Some residents went to school on site; cookery, child care and fashion classes complemented the National Curriculum subjects. Classes were small and the teachers female.

Magenta saw itself as a national resource for adolescents who had failed in other settings. Of the six young women in Central House, there were two sisters who had been involved in prostitution, three came from psychiatric hospitals and one had a history of violence, drug abuse and truancy in other care placements. All had signed an agreement allowing staff to control their behaviour. As the alternatives to Magenta were secure units or hospital placements, their choice was restricted.

'Vulnerable women' was the term used by the manager to describe the group of divorcees or single parents in their mid years who were often employed as carers. The salary was set slightly in excess of wages at the local supermarket. An unqualified staff team of seven was supported by the manager and a visiting clinical psychologist who struggled to reconcile his desire to care for the residents with the need to control and motivate the staff.

*Yellow*

Yellow was established by a voluntary agency to provide respite care for children with disabilities. Up to five children of the 40 served by the home could be resident in the carefully adapted bungalow at any one time. They usually stayed for only a few days. Colours, music, fabric textures, pictures, toys and books were selected to appeal to the range of children's abilities. The staff explained, 'the children must want to come here'. The staff team of 14 had been together, with only one change, since the home opened four years prior to the fieldwork for this research. Eleven had experience of raising their own children and three of caring for children with disabilities. They appeared devoted to their work, friendly and supportive. On the other hand, none was qualified in social work although three had nursing certificates.

Residents comprised boys and girls aged 5 to 18 years. They had a variety of learning and physical disabilities and several also displayed challenging behaviour. Problems were continually discussed, whether in staff meetings or with families who were universally seen as integral to the work of the home. Many of the children knew one another via school and the older teenagers enjoyed the opportunities to meet socially at the home. The mix of residents was carefully considered by parents and staff together.

*Cyan*

The final home was one part of a large therapeutic community providing places for 80 children in the wing of an historic mansion. Considerable effort had been taken to make the surroundings suitable for 10 children. Most residents attended the community's school 200 yards away. They were taught in small classes by specialist teachers and were encouraged to move to local mainstream schools when it was felt they were ready. There was a striking amount of contact between care staff and the teachers. Four times daily children passed between school and 'home' and information on their mood, effort and attitude was exchanged by care staff and teachers.

Most of the nine children in Cyan displayed behaviours associated with previous abuse, some had suffered loss or death of a family member and all had experienced several failed placements. They came from several local authorities, some a considerable distance from the home, and were expecting to stay for several years. The therapeutic approach stressed the importance of the 'group'; children thus knew one another's problems and were encouraged to display mutual concern and affection. Naturally, there were rivalries within the group but physical violence was rare. At first sight, it appeared that residents knew why they were placed at this home and sensed that Cyan was able to help them.

Nine staff were employed to look after the children, although relief could be obtained from the other living units of the therapeutic community in the event of sickness. Staff worked long hours, often over 70 a week, and could often be found after the shift had ended discussing the day's events, being supervised or just generally winding down. There was little time or energy for a private life; as one staff member said, 'you live here and go home for a break'. Seven of the nine were in their 20s, single and in their first child care post. Only one had a social work qualification but all received regular 'in house' training which could lead to a recognised diploma. This certainly helped produce a consistency of approach and a belief in what could be achieved.

## Conclusion

Nine homes were selected to give a representative picture of residential homes for children looked after in England and Wales. The 65 children living in these establishments when the fieldwork began were supported by roughly twice as many care staff. The overwhelming impression from visiting these places was the variety of provision, the lack of qualifications but considerable commitment of staff and the obscure view of the needs of residents. The task of this study is to break down these first impressions and make sense of what was happening in these nine homes with the purpose of explaining why some do better than others in achieving good outcomes for children.

This chapter has described the homes as they appeared when the fieldwork began. Over the following year each changed as staff and children arrived and left and policies altered. The next chapter considers these developments.

# 5 How the homes changed

The nine homes in the study have been described to give a sense of the atmosphere within their walls and of their potential strengths and weaknesses at the start of the fieldwork. Subsequently much more was learned. Residential homes are not static and to understand them fully, they need to be visited over a period of time. When looking at the movement of staff, the arrival and departure of children or alterations to the fabric, aims and philosophy of a home, patterns emerge that may not be apparent on a single visit.

The prospect of change can be threatening but in the nine homes it was also found to have benefits. Even those that ran smoothly and met their stated aims constantly sought evaluation to avoid the risk of stagnation. The search for stability did not obviate a self-critical and questioning approach. In the context of contemporary children's services, it is almost a *sine qua non* for residential homes to be forward looking, adaptable and flexible. Legislation and child care principles may be relatively constant, but the characteristics of staff and children, the administrative systems and practice expectations are not.

Residential homes need to be outward as well as forward looking. The reporting of events in Staffordshire and Leicestershire in the early 1990s and in North Wales more recently revealed gross abuse of children in residential care. These incidents emphasise the benefits of wider scrutiny from outside professionals and the local community, whether for purpose of management, advice or befriending. In the past, young people and staff have not felt safe to air their grievances and report bad practice. Similarly, residential care for children has not been sure of its place within the network of child care services. As explained, the perspective encouraged by the *Children Act*, 1989 views children's residential homes as just one possible part of the range of services local authorities must provide.

The effectiveness of the homes in this study will be viewed in the context of change over time. Regular research visits over the period of a year meant that patterns of change and their effect on the individual homes could be studied. In attempts to understand and explain such patterns, it was important first to distinguish the different dimensions of change in children's homes. At the outset, this was done by separating the home into its main components:

- The building; that is, the physical environment.
- The individuals within, primarily the children, staff and manager.
- The philosophy, the aims and objectives, as expressed, for example, in what is often termed the 'statement of purpose and function'.

## Physical environment

Most homes experienced some changes to the physical environment and in one, Cyan, the group moved house. Working under the umbrella of a therapeutic community, they were given the opportunity to transfer to a specially designed building a few miles away from the main site, out of the corner section of the old mansion house that had been 'home' to Cyan residents for half a century. Most of the children resident at the time the study began had lived at Cyan for a number of years. For many it was the longest period of stability and security they had experienced. The move was potentially very unsettling and had to be carefully planned and co-ordinated.

The children were introduced to the idea while the new house was being built and regular visits took place during its various stages of development. The children were also allowed to make decisions about the house encouraging a degree of 'ownership', for example in the choice of bedroom and its decor. Much attention was paid to making the house colourful and child friendly, even to the extent that an experienced interior designer was dismissed because she could not satisfy the manager that the child's perspective would be accommodated. After the move, staff worked hard to maintain familiar routines and to provide a general sense of stability and consistency for the children.

Changes to the physical environment and fabric of the home were of a different nature at Indigo. Despite the threats of Gary at the dinner table described in the previous chapter, the initial visit found an attractive house, colourfully decorated and well resourced, with its own music room, games area and television lounge. Clearly a lot of effort had gone into the layout and interior design. Over the following year, the house deteriorated and, at the time of the final visit, was a sorry shadow of its former self. Numerous items of furniture had been broken and not replaced; after a number of repeat performances, staff felt there was little point. Decorations during the festive season were few and far between, the feeling being that they would be ripped down as soon as they were put up. Interest in the music room and games room declined and they were usually to be found locked and out of bounds. Items, such as a television belonging to one of the residents, were sold by the young people to pay for drugs.

These illustrations contrast ways the physical environment and fabric of a home can change. One was carefully managed so that the potential for unnecessary disruption to the lives of already unsettled children was avoided. The second represents a steady and unmanaged decline, indicating wider problems. The other seven centres experienced change somewhere between these extremes, with two, Red and Orange, temporarily moving elsewhere while redecoration took place and others benefiting from or enduring degrees of improvement or deterioration in their surroundings.

## The individuals within the home

Changes to the composition of the people living and working in a home potentially involve children, staff and managers. The extent of changes to the composition of the child group ranged from Cyan where only one child left to be replaced by another during the year to four homes (Yellow, Red, Green and Blue) where levels of turnover were high throughout. The diagram on the next page depicts child group changes during the study period, showing those with the highest and lowest levels of movement.

With the exception of Orange, which was similar to Cyan, there were high levels of turnover. This reflects, in part, the growing use of residential care for short term placements but it also reveals a relatively high incidence of breakdown; 11 of the 65 children at the beginning of the study left prematurely. Depending on the aims of the home, high turnover can potentially unsettle other residents. In five of the nine homes a core group of youngsters (a minimum of three children who had been living together for at least four months) was maintained amidst changes to the group on the periphery.

There were also changes in the composition of staff groups. White and Red had several workers who had been together for some considerable time, for example three of the White team had worked together for 20 years. They knew each other's ways of working and communication was informal, involving little paperwork. All but one of the 14 staff at Yellow had worked together in the three years since the home was established. These stable staff groups tended to endure over the 12 months of fieldwork.

In contrast, Orange, Indigo and Cyan had several resignations and appointments. At the beginning of the study, Orange was entering a period of restructuring into a system of group management with another home. Staff were asked to apply for their own and each other's posts, a process that lasted for several months. In the event, half of the staff from the two homes concerned moved from one to the other. Needless to say, this caused confusion, not least among the children who could not understand why their 'key worker' suddenly preferred to go and look after somebody else.

Diagram 5.1: Frequency of change of children in the homes during the 12 months of study

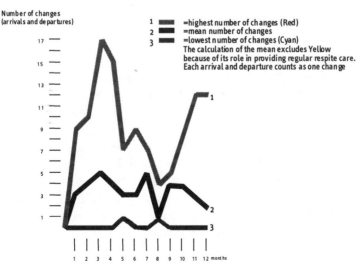

Indigo also worked under a system of group management and the dispirited staff team were keen to get a transfer over to their sister home whenever possible. A number of staff also left residential work altogether during the year. As sickness levels remained high throughout the year, the manager regularly had to call in relief staff. At Cyan, the nature of change was rather different. Some young, inexperienced staff simply burned out and quickly left. The following diagram illustrates the range of staff changes in the nine study homes.

Diagram 5.2: Frequency of change among staff in the nine study homes

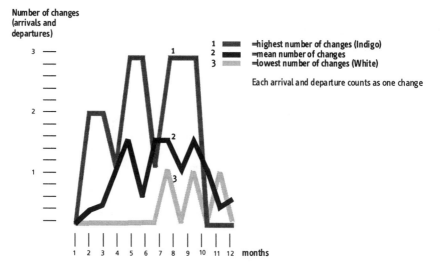

Only Green and Magenta changed manager during the study year. At Green, Jill, who had been in charge for eight years, moved on to manage two other homes in the same locality. Her replacement kept an eye on Green from a distance so, in effect, a newly promoted assistant manager became responsible for the day to day running of the establishment. He had worked at Green prior to completing a Diploma in Social Work and had much enthusiasm for his new role.

Jill had built up a stable staff team over her eight years, although she was considered by some to be controlling and stifling of new ideas. The new assistant manager, in contrast, encouraged staff to use their initiative and put a lot of energy into working with and motivating the home's three distinct staff teams. This change in style seemed to reap benefits. New activities were arranged by the staff for the children, including a drama group, a girls' keep fit group and a summer club. At the time of the researchers' last visit, the staff were busy writing and arranging a Christmas pantomime. The new manager also facilitated training in relevant issues such as child sexual abuse. This had the effect of increasing staff knowledge and nurturing a stronger belief in what the home could achieve.

There were less significant management changes in other homes. In Blue, the manager was seconded to a Diploma in Social Work course and replaced by her two assistants. At Red a new manager, also responsible for a second home, took over several months after the post had been vacated due to the previous incumbent's promotion. In effect this made little difference to the daily running of the home which was already well directed by the two assistant managers and offered no challenge to the routines of other staff.

## Philosophy, aims and objectives

The most significant changes to the aims and objectives of a home occurred at Green. Mid-way through the study period, prior to the change in manager, its purpose altered from time-limited (up to six months) care for children with diverse needs to medium or long term (over six months) provision for 'vulnerable children', defined more specifically as 'those who have suffered abuse or have moderate learning difficulties'. In practice, this meant it accommodated increasing numbers of children with needs associated with past sexual abuse, which included some boys who were at risk of displaying sexually abusive behaviour themselves. It also meant that the characteristics of the resident population were noticeably different on the second visit. As would be expected, abuse histories were more common but more children had also been separated from home for longer periods before entry, had committed offences and had broken down in foster care. A compensation was that more admissions were well planned. The new statement gave greater clarity to its role but posed new care problems.

Blue also underwent a major change. Having been a long-term unit preparing younger residents for fostering and adoption, it became a resource preparing adolescents for independence. As with Green, this led to changes in the residents' background histories. On the second visit, the recent arrivals tended to be older, to have been looked after for shorter periods but to have been admitted in emergency. This new remit was met by the staff with uncertainty. Daily routines changed; eight o'clock bedtimes were no longer appropriate, for example, and the previously communal mealtimes became a hit and miss affair, dependent on which young people chose to be home and eat with the group. Staff were expected to deal with unfamiliar tasks, such as how to respond to residents who wished to stay out all night.

The effects of insecurity generated by these changes were mitigated by a constant process of readjustment at Blue. Several of the children who had been at the home for a number of years and had grown into adolescents stayed on and formed a core group. The stability of the staff group ensured that everyone knew one another's ways of working and, despite a crisis early on, were able to act together to find solutions to new problems. They set up group discussions and training sessions on working with adolescents. A new role was created for a member of staff trained in facilitating the transition of young people to live in the community. The new statement of aims and objectives was further refined to accommodate the views of staff.

Although changes in the building, individuals and philosophy have been discussed separately, they can coalesce. A change in one dimension can produce a knock-on effect in another. Green illustrates this point. The change of manager led to modifications in the general philosophy of the home and ushered in a new interior decor. Under the original manager, Green lacked colour and had a drab, old fashioned feel. On her departure the atmosphere changed, with colourful, youth friendly posters and pictures appearing on the walls. Any funds that could be spared were used to modernise the decor of the big house.

At Magenta, the new manager also brought a new set of priorities. Although the written statement of aims and objectives was not altered, adaptations were made to the home's general approach. The previous incumbent, a clinical psychologist by training, had been viewed from above as too concerned with the individual well-being of his staff team to be an efficient manager. His replacement was more concerned with material than emotional well-being and pursued generous salary increases and staff benefits. Under the new manager Magenta felt increasingly like a business venture with all the benefits - clarity of management - and weaknesses - less focus on the needs of the child - that followed.

## Issues raised by changes in children's homes

### Management of change

Observing the way the nine homes developed, it became clear that the management of change is as important as change itself. It was possible for major alterations to be handled so that they achieved maximum benefit with minimum disruption and for minor changes to produce great unsettlement. At Cyan moving house could have been traumatic, but the effects were nearly all positive. Despite initial anxieties, the staff group were supported by management and came to see the potential benefits of the move. They and the children were involved in the design of the new house and watched it being built; all along it promised to be an appealing place to live and work. For the children it was a chance to show that they could make this move and still be safe. Inevitably there were some problems. One child in particular 'kicked out' and caused quite costly damage to the new house and the group's car. However, the adults worked hard to 'hold' the children through this transition, maintaining consistency of approach and familiar routines. The approach paid dividends and the outcome, in the sense of a treatment programme being maintained, was good.

Yellow had, *de facto*, to deal with continuing changes of the child group. As a respite home, new children came daily. A striking feature of the home was how carefully staff managed this routine. They knew all the children well, put great effort into planning the mix of residents and ensured that children were allowed a sense of ownership of and belonging to the home even though their stay was brief. Each child had a photograph and name plate hung on the door of the bedroom allocated to them before their arrival. Similarly their favourite posters would find a place on the bedroom wall in time for their stay.

At Indigo five of the original group of six young people moved on during the year and once Gary, the particularly problematic young man, had departed, the local authority quickly filled the home to its full capacity. Consequently, no core group of children familiar with the routines of Indigo ever existed. Children coming in on remand were not unusual and emergency placements became the rule rather than the exception.

The staff did not cope well with these changes. By the end of the study, none of the children was attending any form of school and they turned their noses up at alternative entertainment offered by the staff.

Lack of occupation led to them finding their own amusements and incidents of offending and drug misuse became commonplace. Within the home, levels of violence to staff increased, as did the number of restraint incidents. If the young people were not offending when they arrived at Indigo, they had often graduated to this status by the time they left. The outcome for a substantial number (a third of the children who left the home during the year) was a move on to secure accommodation.

The increased number of restraint incidents might have been managed differently if weary staff had been inclined or encouraged to step back and look at what was happening. Simple questions such as where the incidents were taking place, with whom and what were the potential triggers would have helped. They saw the problem as the children's behaviour; outside observers saw the problem as managing the change of clientele using the home.

Although some change is inevitable and in many circumstances desirable, some sense of continuity and stability is important for children who often have previous experiences marked by considerable disruption. Whatever their length of stay in residence, a fair and consistent approach is to be preferred. Maintaining core groups of children and staff within homes so that a group of people familiar with the routines of the home are available is one way of achieving this but it is not always possible in a home whose remit is to cater for short-term placements. Other ways include having clearly defined aims and objectives, routines, expectations and boundaries which can be easily communicated to each newly arriving child and member of staff.

But, it is also clear from this evidence that no matter how hard homes try, they find it difficult to provide stability for children. Of the 65 young people resident at the start of the study, 24 were still there a year later, all of them in six of the nine homes. Although these young people had lived in the same place, in that 12 month period they collectively experienced: one change of location, one temporary move to another site, two changes in the statement of purpose and function of the home and two changes of emphasis. In addition, there were over 50 staff and 200 child arrivals and departures. Consistency and stability for a child can be achieved by placing a child in residential care but doing so is inherently difficult because of the state of flux in many homes.

## Homes that were in need of change but stayed the same

Throughout the study period, it was not uncommon to find elements of a home that required change. Three (Orange, Indigo and White), for example, had aims and objectives that were clearly outdated and ineffective, and had been so for quite some time. Orange was established to work 'therapeutically' with vulnerable and damaged children but none of the staff was appropriately trained and 'vulnerable and damaged' was never defined. Maybe this left staff, as they claimed, 'set up to fail'. There was a need either to employ new staff or set more realistic aims and objectives.

White claimed to offer accommodation for children for up to six months, yet a cursory look at the files showed that half of the children had been there for at least a year, if not two. At Indigo, a lack of any clearly defined remit meant staff were expected to take in children with a plethora of needs, many of which they felt ill-equipped to deal with. So called 'statements of purpose and function' are not set in stone; homes always need to be flexible to respond to the changing needs of children looked after. The more the statement is relevant, achievable and generally understood by staff and children alike, the more likely it is that positive change will be effected.

Situations where children were ready to move but could not were also indicative of an overdue need for change. The tendency to allow children to drift, especially if they are not causing too many problems, still dogs residential care. Young people become stuck and miss key opportunities. In White, a number of children who had entered under respite care arrangements were still living there two years on. The results from the application of the *Looking After Children* materials confirm this, fortunately not in the extreme sense of the forgotten children described by Lambert and Rowe a quarter of a century ago but in terms of poor inter-agency co-ordination and neglect of education, health and family relationships. Staff too can get 'stuck in a rut'. Although having a team of individuals who have worked together for some time has obvious benefits, it can equally lead to rigidity, suspicion of change and continuing bad practice. The injection of new blood and fresh enthusiasm into the existing core of staff is to be encouraged.

## Conclusion

All nine homes studied changed to some degree throughout the 12 months of fieldwork and the nature of change was complex in some. These results can be assimilated into three patterns. First were those homes that were forward looking and progressing or consistently working well. Three homes matched this pattern - Cyan, Yellow and Red. Second were those homes that fluctuated throughout the year but managed to maintain overall ideals, aims and objectives. They had times of crisis but managed to work through them successfully. This pattern was also found in three homes - White, Blue and Green. Third were those homes that deteriorated, gradually losing sense of their aims and purpose. This pattern describes Indigo and Orange. These three patterns account for eight of the nine homes. The ninth, Magenta, was difficult to place, and its position as an exception (in statistical terms an 'outlier') in the study will be discussed in the next chapter.

The extent and effects of the actual developments were varied; in one a minor modification to a shift system seemed to paralyse staff, whereas in another a major relocation was achieved without undue distress. Yet if homes are to respond sensitively to the needs of children some change is inevitable.

Several points emerge from these findings that are relevant to child care policy and practice. First, it is often stated that the insecurities expressed by residential staff stem from fears of redundancy or of child abuse investigations. Yet, in none of the homes studied did these issues arise; there was a lot of change but it did not concern closure or scandal. It is true that in two homes staff had to reapply for their jobs and in one other there was talk of closure but, while these situations created obvious anxiety, neither posed a serious threat. Second, none of the changes observed seemed to be driven by an overarching local authority plan for looked after children based on needs assessments of children in the whole community. They were all opportunist reactions to having a resource available or attempts to make the facilities meet some perceived need. These needs were defined to fit the resource rather than the reverse with the result that there was endless patching up and redesigning of the system.

This situation had two effects. It meant that the changes were not informed by *Children Act* principles but by organisational restructuring or reactions to acute problems. None of the changes described reflects a shift to partnership with parents, a reduction in delay, better planning or greater sensitivity to users' views. Indeed, none of the pressures for change seemed to emanate from the children or their families. Neither did the changes indicate moves to better inter-agency planning or a more complementary role for residential care in the careers of looked after children.

The weakness exposed by this chapter is the lack of any sense of a 'treatment' service. Facilities are so closely tied to buildings that any focus on the needs of the child and an effective range of services to meet them is severely circumscribed. It is like the worst aspects of debates about hospital reorganisation where fabric becomes inseparable from treatment. This may not be a problem in short-term planning, as services can be quickly reshaped, but it augurs less well for the development of evidence based social work when ways of service delivery are viewed so rigidly. Could, for example, one still entertain the suggestion that arrested the 1989 De Haan International Conference on residential child care; namely that as policy changes have led to fewer but more sophisticated units helping children who need the services provided, the most radical contribution of residential care to child welfare over the past 50 years is that four fifths of it has closed?

The contribution of this study however is to concentrate less on the changes themselves and more on how and why homes develop in the way that they do. Why did not Orange behave in the same way as Cyan, which has similar therapeutic aims and objectives? Why did Red prosper with its unpromising recruits of predominantly 16 year old boys recently thrown out of home, foster care or other residential placements while Indigo, with its multi-disciplinary and well trained staff, backed by a bank of relief carers, continued to deteriorate? Could it be explained as a failure of management? Was the wrong leader appointed? Did they recruit the wrong staff? Was it anything to do with the building?

In Chapter Two the concepts of structure and culture were introduced to take the analysis forward. The nine institutions will now be re-scrutinised using these perspectives, the aim being to see how far they explain the findings presented in the last two chapters and, later, whether they relate to good welfare outcomes for children.

# 6 The structure of homes

The previous chapter charted patterns of change within the nine homes, begging an explanation of which factors make for progress rather than steady deterioration. Early on, the idea was introduced that the key to understanding the process and nature of change in homes may lie somewhere in the relationship between the structure of a home and the culture of its staff and child groups. The starting point to any exploration of this relationship, if it exists, must be the structural aspects of the homes.

The structure of a home was defined earlier as 'an orderly arrangement of social relations and continuing arrangements of kinds of people, governed by a concept of proper behaviour in their relations with each other'. Further discussion led to a distinction being made between the societal, formal and belief goals of residential centres and a need to understand the relationship between them.

The *societal* goals are those shared principles and ideas about the way children are raised, including children in need. Those that relate specifically to children's residential care are manifest in legislation, particularly the *Children Act*, 1989; residential care is an essential part of the continuum of services under Part III of the legislation that sets out what a local authority must do to support and protect vulnerable children. Volume Four of the guidance accompanying the 1989 Act deals specifically with residential care. These societal goals were largely unchanging over the year of study.

The *formal* goals are the aims and objectives of each children's home and, therefore, represent some interpretation of the societal goals to meet local conditions and the particular needs of the children being served. These goals are usually written down in what is typically called the home's 'statement of purpose and function', but they may also be expressed through clear and careful communication between the head of home and his or her staff. Ideally, both conditions will apply. It is little use, for example, if a home has well thought through aims and objectives beautifully set out on paper if they are not applied in practice. Similarly, a manager who clearly expresses formal goals but never writes them down may create a healthy environment while he or she is in post only to create confusion and ambiguity on leaving.

The final set of goals encompasses what a manager fundamentally *believes* about what the home can do for its residents, including the capability of the staff. Understanding the managers' beliefs about residential care and their homes, and seeing whether these beliefs are concordant with the societal and formal goals of the homes became an important indicator of performance as the study progressed. Does the manager believe that his or her home has a positive role to play in the lives of the children it cares for or, like so many charged with this responsibility, is it simply a place for children to be dumped, to be sheltered by inadequate staff in unsuitable surroundings?

Getting an accurate picture of a manager's beliefs is not, of course, as straightforward as charting societal or formal goals. What the manager says is one thing but this has to be checked against how he or she behaves. Considered in context, any of the following might indicate a manager's belief goals: his or her absence through sickness, whether she or he chooses to eat with the staff and children, whether she or he is prepared to put in any time over and above shift hours, and whether relevant research is read or other services visited. By observing these factors it was possible to see if the manager was committed to the job and whether he or she was prepared to make sacrifices for it. Interactions between the manager, staff and children were also carefully charted. Off the cuff comments such as 'we are sent the wrong type of children', for example, could, again in context, be illuminating.

These societal, formal and belief goals were analysed in each residential centre, thus giving a picture of the structure of the home which included any concordance or discord between the goals. The details of that analysis will emerge during the remainder of the study. There will be quantitative work adding up and cross-tabulating factors and qualitative insights from those living and working in the homes. Eventually, the aim is to produce methods for managers to test the results in their own setting. Here, however, the requirement is for a simple description of what happened in the residential centres studied and this may best be done by setting out an ideal type for the structure of a children's home and then comparing how each of the nine described in the preceding chapter fared against this benchmark.

## Towards an ideal structure

The structure of a home should work in the best interests of the children sheltered. Three conditions relating to the way the three types of structural goals interact need to be met in order to achieve this. First, the societal goals represent the overarching principles and values governing the way children are raised in our society and, as such, they form an umbrella under which all children's homes should fit. It is important, therefore, that the formal goals of each home are based on and work within these societal goals. Of the societal goals determined by the *Children Act*, 1989, for example, there are key principles that prevail, such as the importance of working in partnership with parents and of a local authority acting as a reasonable parent to the children it looks after. The formal goals of a children's home should not conflict with these principles; any statement made about the standard of care provided within the home, for example, should be in line with the standard expected from a 'reasonable parent'.

As the societal goals form a conceptual framework and set of principles within which all the homes should operate (and a baseline against which to measure formal and belief goals), their adequacy is of the utmost importance. The *Children Act*, 1989 is a well respected legal instrument which was significantly influenced by research findings on how best to serve the interests of children in need. In time, it may be superseded by new law influenced by further research and those operating in other countries will currently be working in a different context. Whatever the situation, in this model societal goals are the starting point.

Second, formal goals should be well thought through and clearly expressed. It is important for all those who work and live in a residential home to be clear about what the responsible organisation is setting out to achieve. In addition to being well defined, formal goals should be achievable; the home's resources, such as money, staff and levels of training should be adequate to meet its formal goals. If a home sets itself up as a centre of expertise for counselling abused children and doing work with their families but has nobody on the staff who knows what this means let alone how it might be delivered, it is unlikely to be successful in meeting its formal goals. Clarity of purpose and a realistic set of goals are therefore essential ingredients in the smooth running of a residential home.

Third, the belief goals, as expressed by the manager, should be concordant with the formal goals. If the formal goals state, for example, that the home seeks to provide respite care for children with disabilities, then the manager's expressed beliefs should reflect this formally defined purpose. If the manager's belief is that the children should be rescued from their parents or that respite exacerbates rather than eases parents' problems, thus demonstrating some discord between formal and belief goals, the quality of care in the home and therefore outcome for the children will suffer. When such contradictions become enshrined in rhetoric, with phrases like 'residential care is abusive to staff' becoming common talk even when the implications of such claims are misunderstood, an even wider gap between formal and belief dimensions will open up, suggesting greater problems for the home.

So, one ideal scenario would be to match the societal goal that a children's home should act as a reasonable parent with the complementary formal goal for it to provide a stable, caring environment which meets residents' primary needs; this situation would bring the societal and formal dimensions into concordance. If the manager believed in these goals and felt the home was able effectively to meet the children's needs and there was no reason based upon research observation and other evidence to bring the beliefs into question, then the three structural goals could be described as concordant.

This ideal type can be expressed in a diagram. A home that maintained consistently accordant relationships between its structural goals throughout the year would have the following pattern:

Diagram 6.1: Consistently concordant relationship between societal, formal and belief goals

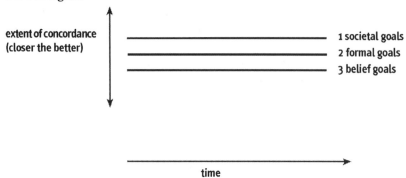

In contrast, the relationships between societal, formal and belief goals in a home that had a consistently discordant structure would display the following pattern:

Diagram 6.2: Consistently discordant relationship between societal, formal and belief goals

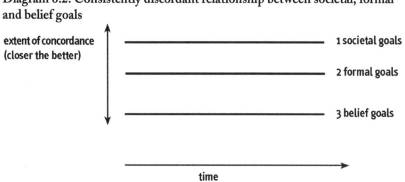

These two contrasting illustrations are unlikely to be typical of real children's homes and the reader may be taken aback by the simplicity of the approach. They do, though, provide a baseline against which the performance of the nine homes studied can be measured. Moreover, the method of analysis should make it possible both to illustrate and then to explain the patterns of change in the study homes outlined in the previous chapter. It will be recalled that three categories of home emerged; first the homes that were forward looking and progressing or consistently working well, second those that fluctuated but kept abreast of their overall aims and objectives, third, the generally deteriorating.

## Homes that are forward looking and progressing or consistently working well

Cyan serves as a good illustration of such a home. Here the three types of structural goals were closely concordant. The societal goals remained constant throughout the study and applied equally to all the homes involved. The formal goals at Cyan were not only well articulated but were also based on and worked within the wider philosophy of the therapeutic community to which they belonged. It has to be said that, although some of these ideas are discussed in the psychotherapeutic literature, they are not always presented in a way that staff or managers can easily understand. The primary formal goal was to provide long term, therapeutic care in a small, stable group-living environment. Education was provided in the on-site school with a curriculum tailored to each child's individual needs. Emphasis was placed on the importance of the children building good, stable relationships with a warm, caring group of staff. Contact between the child and his or her family was maintained, even when children were several hundred miles from their natural home. Therapy, however, was exclusive to the child. All of this was clearly communicated by the manager to her staff.

Overall these formal goals incorporate and work within overarching societal goals but there was some gap apparent with regard to the emphasis in the *Children Act*, 1989 on the importance of working in partnership with parents. At the beginning of the study, staff in Cyan generally viewed children's families as baleful, perhaps understandably, considering the abuse the children had often suffered while living at home. But a research study which charted the experiences of leavers demonstrated that most leavers from Cyan eventually went home, had an influence. By the end of the study year, contact levels between parents and children had increased and there was a greater emphasis on the importance of working with families. It would have been preferable for Cyan's formal goals to have been written down because, as many of the other units in this therapeutic community had found to their cost, good performance tended to rely too heavily on the abilities of individual managers and rapid deterioration often followed their departure.

The manager's beliefs mirrored her expressed formal goals for the home. There were no areas of discord apparent. She spent a great deal of time at the children's home, including many hours over and above her allocated shifts. Very active in the home, she ate with the children and staff, played with the children and involved herself in the day to day routines of the home. Overall she demonstrated great commitment to Cyan and consistently sacrificed personal time for the home's benefit when she felt it necessary.

There was nothing in her approach or rhetoric to suggest any areas of tension between the home's formal goals and her belief goals. She was realistic about what could be achieved with such 'damaged children' but did not use these limitations as an excuse to abandon all effort. Occasionally, she voiced concerns that the work was too demanding on the staff who put in extremely long hours and great commitment and made sacrifices in their personal lives for the job. But this, too, was a realistic assessment of the home's weakness and did not divert from the slow process of therapeutic work.

The interaction between the societal, formal and belief goals at Cyan was generally complementary. Areas of conflict were minimal; for example insufficient stress was initially placed on working with families within a set of formal goals that were otherwise comprehensive. A similar picture emerges when the other two homes from the forward looking category are considered. At both Red and Yellow the three structural goals were closely in line with one another, and in all three homes this concordant relationship lasted throughout the study year, with little apparent wavering.

Diagram 6.3: Concordance of goals at Red, Yellow and Cyan

|        | S, F, B goals concordant | Areas of discord /ambiguity apparent | Discordant S, F and B goals |
|--------|:---:|:---:|:---:|
| Red    | ✓ | | |
| Yellow | ✓ | | |
| Cyan   | ✓ | | |

## Fluctuating homes

Green was typical of the homes that fluctuated but kept abreast of their overall aims and objectives. At the beginning of the study, the formal goals were written in the home's statement of purpose and function. However, the remit was very wide and the goals lacked clear expression. They aimed to cater for 12 children, aged 11-17, for a limited period (up to six months). The home stated it would cater for children from a wide range of backgrounds; their reasons for admission varied from those described as 'at risk', to those classed as 'beyond parental control', to young people on remand awaiting trial. Broad statements were made about the importance of education, and the need to provide children with 'good parent' figures, but clear indicators as to how these aims were to be achieved were absent. This lack of clarity meant that the home provided for a grey area of need rather than defining a positive role for itself in the continuum of the local authority's provision.

The head of home's belief goals reflected the ambiguous formal goals. She spoke of the importance of providing containment and shelter for the children and of ensuring that each received education but she, too, was limited in her ability to express how those goals were to be achieved. Watching her around the home, it was clear that while generally committed to the children, she ignored techniques most suitable for children's needs. For example, she failed to utilise staff skills fully and she did not involve them in the resolution of perceived problems. She tended to rule by decree, fostering an atmosphere of 'keep your head down and get the job done'. The poor communication meant that the societal goal to provide 'good parenting' clashed with her behaviour, which suggested she believed that staff lacked 'good parenting' skills. She failed to encourage a consistency of approach and shared beliefs among carers, which are pre-conditions of achieving 'good parenting'.

An exploration of the relationship between the three types of structural goals at Green revealed that, although the formal and belief dimensions were relatively close, there was some ambiguity as to the role of the home, leading to areas of tension with societal goals. This pattern was similar in the two other homes in the fluctuating category. Uncertainty about definition of the formal goals and the ability of staff to meet them was an obvious difficulty. The staff generally managed to provide a warm, caring environment for the young people they looked after, but lacked clarity as to what they were actually seeking to do.

At Blue, staff struggled to adapt to their new remit of working with adolescents. White staff felt the formally defined goals were outdated and unhelpful; they did not seem relevant to the tasks that they faced. For instance, one young person had been there for more than two years and another two for a year, despite the written statement that children would stay for relatively short periods. The managers at both homes became disillusioned working in a context over which they felt they had little control.

In Green, Blue and White areas of tension between the three types of structural goals were evident. Adding these homes to the earlier diagram gives the following:

Diagram 6.4: Concordance of goals at Red, Yellow, Cyan, Green, Blue and White

|  | S, F, B goals concordant | Areas of discord /ambiguity apparent | Discordant S, F and B goals |
|---|---|---|---|
| Red | ✓ |  |  |
| Yellow | ✓ |  |  |
| Cyan | ✓ |  |  |
| Green |  | ✓ |  |
| Blue |  | ✓ |  |
| White |  | ✓ |  |

## Deteriorating homes

The most problematic of the nine homes participating in the study was Indigo. Here the formal goals were again insufficiently defined, leaving staff unprepared to deal with children from a wide range of backgrounds. Indigo aimed to provide stability and an alternative home for children unable to live with their family but only, supposedly, for a few months. The goals were too vague in expression and focus, particularly with regard to how long children should stay or where they should go next. Rather than defining a constructive role, the home responded as best as it could to whatever came along. As a consequence, some children remained there far longer than had been intended, lacking any positive plans for the future.

The manager believed Indigo to be more than capable of providing a stable, warm environment for most children 'in need'. However, particularly difficult young people, whom they could not control, were sent to them. Staff found they were unable to make these young people go to school, give up drugs or stop offending. Thus, the manager concluded that she had been set an 'impossible task' and had been sent the 'wrong type' of children, many of whom in her view should be locked up. She viewed the home overall as a 'dumping ground' for the local authority. Her belief goals were discordant with societal goals, in that she appeared to believe it would be difficult to act as a 'reasonable parent' to the 'wrong children'. The view of the children as 'villains' prevented sufficient attention being paid to possible ways of modifying the home's approach to cater for their needs. Overall the picture of the structural goals in play at Indigo shows high levels of discord.

A similar picture emerges at Orange, the second home in the deteriorating category. Their formal goals classed Orange as a 'therapeutic unit' that catered for particularly vulnerable children. The manager expressed the belief that the home could provide the children with a stable placement, but that it was unable to provide therapy. She also made occasional comments which intimated that by failing to provide her with appropriately trained staff, the local authority was 'setting them up to fail'. She doubted whether the home could even achieve stability in many cases. So, at Orange they had an inappropriately defined formal purpose and significant gaps were evident between their formal and belief goals.

To complete the earlier diagram, the situation of these two homes at the beginning of the study period would be represented by the following categories:

Diagram 6.5: Concordance of goals in eight homes

| | S, F, B goals concordant | Areas of discord/ ambiguity apparent | Discordant S, F and B goals |
|---|---|---|---|
| Red | ✓ | | |
| Yellow | ✓ | | |
| Cyan | ✓ | | |
| Blue | | ✓ | |
| Green | | ✓ | |
| White | | ✓ | |
| Orange | | | ✓ |
| Indigo | | | ✓ |

## Magenta: an exception

Of all the homes, Magenta did not fit easily into any of the three categories. In many ways it offered an impressive package - a long-term placement catering to individual needs and with education on site for girls who would otherwise find themselves in secure accommodation.

The education was certainly impressive and the small group of female teaching staff worked successfully with the girls, offering a good range of subjects and extra-curricular activities. Girls who had been out of the education system for some time found themselves regularly attending school again.

The area where flaws were most evident in Magenta's approach was in its attempts to meet the range of needs which the girls displayed. They came to Magenta having usually experienced numerous unsuccessful care placements. The managers of the Magenta venture were proud of their claim that they rarely turned any of these girls away. What this meant, in fact, was that the girls displayed behaviour problems such as eating disorders, precocious sexual activity and arson, some of which required psychiatric oversight, but the 'care staff' responsible for meeting such a range of needs were generally inexperienced and untrained. Management quite openly said that wages were set below professional rates. Although Magenta had its own training programme for new staff, this was pitched at a basic level, and was insufficient to meet the plethora or depth of needs that the girls presented.

The change of management of Magenta, observed in the course of the research, brought a shift in priorities towards greater emphasis on material well being and generous monetary allowances as a means of encouraging the girls to stay. However, this change made little difference to the underlying mismatch between ideology and practice. In theory, Magenta aimed to 're-parent' the girls and to meet their primary needs but in practice the staff were insufficiently equipped to fulfil this.

The study included several girls who came to Magenta but whose needs were not met. A young girl with a severe eating disorder left the placement prematurely for a specialist unit at the local psychiatric hospital after it was discovered that she had reached a dangerously low weight. Of the six girls living at Magenta at the beginning of the study, four left prematurely.

It is difficult to place Magenta into the three categories of change in the homes (progressing, fluctuating or deteriorating) because there were a number of contradictions at play. While the education side of the provision remained consistently good throughout the study, the inadequacy of staff to meet the girls' primary needs was a problem from start to finish. Two different managers with different priorities made little impact on the underlying gap between theory and practice.

The relationship between Magenta's structural goals was similarly complex. There was a gap evident between societal and formal goals due to the home's failure to work with the girls' families. However, in other ways the formal goals, at least on the surface, appeared impressive and based on *Children Act* principles. The manager at the start of the study believed strongly in the importance of 're-parenting' girls and addressing individual needs, but became disillusioned with what he saw as the inadequacy of provision. The new manager was also able to speak clearly about Magenta's ideology. He focused less on the needs of the individual but was in tune with the business ethos of the place. In different ways, the beliefs of both these individuals were, on one level, concordant with formal goals but the fundamental relationship between theory and practice was flawed.

## Change over time

As already discussed, residential homes are not static. Descriptions have been given of the relationship between the three types of structural goals in the residential homes at the beginning of the study. Particular focus has been given to one home in each of these three categories - Cyan, Green and Indigo. The following illustrations show how the structures of these homes changed and considers what effect these shifting relationships had on overall levels of structural accord. The following diagram represents the relationship between the structural goals at Cyan over the year.

**Diagram 6.6: Relationship between structural goals - Cyan**

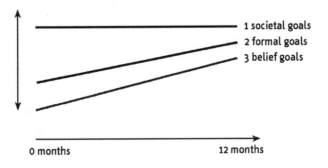

It shows that these goals became closer within a context of generally high concordance. The formal goals became closer to the societal goals with the growing emphasis placed on working with the children's families. The belief line runs in parallel with this formal line because the manager's belief goals throughout the study closely reflected the home's formal goals, which were themselves based largely on her clear expression.

Green, in contrast, illustrates fluctuations in structural patterns. Over the year it underwent two major changes, significantly affecting both the formal and the belief goals. Half way through the study year, a new statement of purpose and function was implemented. The details of this new statement have been described in the previous chapter, but overall the effect was to bring the formal goals into a position of greater concordance with the overriding societal goals. Four months later, the long-standing manager left and the newly promoted assistant took her place. It has already been described how different this new manager was from his predecessor and in effect he brought with him a new set of belief goals. Because of the greater emphasis on improving the staff knowledge on child-care issues, involving them in decisions about the running of the home and incorporating *Children Act* principles, the belief goals at Green moved into greater concordance with the formal and societal goals. The following diagram illustrates the relationship between these structural goals over the twelve months. It shows that by the end of the year the home had developed a concordant structure.

Diagram 6.7: Relationship between structural goals - Green

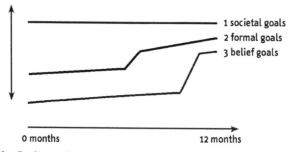

1 societal goals
2 formal goals
3 belief goals

0 months                    12 months

At Indigo the unsatisfactory situation at the outset deteriorated to even lower levels of concordance, with a widening gap between societal, formal and belief goals. The formal goals were too vague from the start and became increasingly inappropriate to meet the needs of the children; the home had to look after a growing number of emergency and remand placements. The belief goals deteriorated correspondingly as the manager increasingly felt that Indigo was being sent the 'wrong children'. The following diagram gives an indication of how distant these structural goals had become by the end of the study.

Diagram 6.8: Relationship between structural goals – Indigo

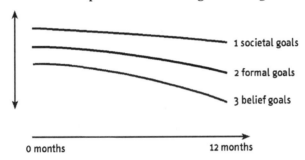

As a result of these changes, at the end of the study year the homes displayed the following structures. Although there is much consistency with the earlier pattern, it can be seen that one home, Green, changed categories. It was described in the previous chapter that it became increasingly reasonably forward looking and progressed well. This corresponds with and is accounted for by the improvement in the relationship between the three types of goals.

Diagram 6.9: Concordance between goals at end of study

|  | S, F, B goals concordant | Areas of discord/ ambiguity apparent | Discordant S, F and B goals |
|---|---|---|---|
| Red | ✓ |  |  |
| Yellow | ✓ |  |  |
| Cyan | ✓ |  |  |
| Blue |  | ✓ |  |
| Green | ✓ |  |  |
| White |  | ✓ |  |
| Orange |  |  | ✓ |
| Indigo |  |  | ✓ |

Membership of the three change categories is explained largely by the nature of the relationship between the three structural goals. The homes with concordant structures were also those that adapted to change successfully and were forward looking and progressing. Those with discontinuous relationships between their structural goals fell into the fluctuating homes category, surviving the changes demanded of them but with some difficulty. The structures of the homes in the deteriorating category were even more discordant by the end of the study period; here change, even when well-intended, only made matters worse.

## Conclusion

This chapter has illustrated the importance of the nature of the relationship between three structural goals. Close concordance between the societal, formal and belief goals of a home provides a favourable context when changes are imposed or the need for change arises. External pressures can be incorporated into internal development plans. Thus concordance has been shown to be associated with homes working consistently well or progressing. Discordance makes things difficult and the experiences of Indigo and Orange show that even the best of intentions can easily be thwarted. Before considering ways of improving troubled or ineffective homes, it may be helpful for people managing and working in them to find a way of ascertaining what the structural goals of a home are, and to determine the nature of any discord. This study has formulated questions which help people to do this. As already explained, it is intended once the research has been satisfactorily reviewed to incorporate these in a practice tool that can be used to assess the 'well-being' of a residential home and to highlight areas where improvement could be made. This approach will be discussed in greater depth in Chapter 10.

If the relationship between a home's structural goals has such an important influence on patterns and effects of change in a home, the next question is whether the nature of a home's structure has an influence on the culture of its staff and child groups. Do changes in a home's structure bring about changes in the culture? The following chapter considers the relationship between the structure of a home and the culture of its staff group, and between the culture of the staff and the cultural response of the child group.

# 7 Staff and child cultures

Structure alone is not sufficient to explain the development of children's homes. The second aspect of residential care explored by the study is culture. A book could be devoted to the definition of culture alone. There is no place for that here, although the discussion in Chapter Two covered some of the conceptual issues. Here, the practical questions of whether or not staff or child cultures exist and, if they do, to what extent they relate to structures and outcomes, are addressed. Several methods were used to identify and understand cultures but, to all intents and purposes, the exploration was to find out if staff and residents responded as a group to selected key tasks. If they did, a culture was said to exist.

To get a rounded view of the life of a home, tasks or events likely to occur regularly in residential care were selected in the five areas used in successive Dartington studies to assess the situation of children in need. These are: living situation, family and social relationships, social and anti-social behaviour, education and employment and physical and psychological health. For example, in living situation, the events included 'a new child arrives at the home' and in the area of health tasks included 'a child complains of stomach-ache and does not want to go to school'. The full list is given in Appendix Three.

If individual children or staff within the group were observed to react in the same way to a task or event, then a cultural response was indicated. As five events or tasks were examined in each of the five areas of the child's life, the strength of both the staff and child culture could be measured on a scale from zero to 25. If there were group responses in 15 or more of the tasks or events a culture was considered to be pervasive and strong. Weak cultures were indicated where less than five tasks or events produced group responses; anything in between was classified as medium.

## Do cultures exist?

There was evidence of a strong staff culture in six of the nine homes. In Orange and Green it was considered to be of medium strength, only in Magenta was it found to be weak. The influence of a staff culture was most apparent with respect to tasks and events to do with education and employment. Even in Magenta, the staff responded as a group when it came to school or work.

The nature of the culture varied considerably. For example, in Indigo, staff accepted with resignation the children's refusal to attend school, welcomed in a day care co-ordinator whose job it was to entertain the children and wasted little effort on finding alternative school places. Non-school attendance soon came to be seen as typical. In Green, in contrast, all staff considered school imperative and any refusal to attend stimulated concerted and comprehensive action; daily school contact was established, meetings with teachers arranged and the child undertook six hours of school work every day until he or she returned. This home had low levels of non-school attendance.

Cultures were least evident in the two areas of physical and psychological health and family and social relationships. Only in Yellow did staff act in a concerted fashion when parents visited. Here, all the child's family were involved in planning their child's stay. Elsewhere, the welcome offered to family members varied, depending upon who was on duty at the time or what else was happening with other residents. Similarly, health checks, appointments and decisions about treatment were mostly dealt with on an *ad hoc* basis.

In contrast to the staff, there was less evidence of child cultures in the homes. The strongest child cultures were found in Cyan. There was some appearance of child cultures in Red, White, Green and Indigo but in the remaining four homes, the children rarely acted cohesively. For example, in Orange, on occasion, in response to a particularly unusual event, such as an extremely violent outburst from a resident, the group might come together either to encourage the violence or to curtail it. Soon after, the group would revert to individual actions and responses. Cohesion here was only fleeting.

When it came to asking children what they do when another resident needs restraining, there was a cultural response from six of the nine homes. Contrary to many lay people's expectations, most children support staff to calm these situations, even when there are difficulties elsewhere in the home. Typically, children kept quiet and out of the way until the crisis passed. Only in Indigo did the group response of shouting, fighting and jeering at staff cause incidents to escalate.

Why was there less evidence of child cultures? One explanation may be that children living in a residential home often have little in common. The stereotypical teenager interested only in pop music, fashion, drugs and sex is probably false. There has been a fragmentation of youth cultures in the general population; working class communities do not necessarily cohere, age bands mean less to young people than they used to and society has become multi-cultural. On top of this, children come to residential care with diverse past experiences, present needs and future aspirations. The likelihood of their sharing a comprehensive set of understandings of particular events is slight and certainly less than for staff who at least have actively chosen to work in residential child care.

In two of the homes, the nature of the task and characteristics of the children significantly reduced the potential for cultures to form. At Yellow the children, as well as often having severe disabilities, stayed only a matter of days. Their ability to form relationships and communicate freely was curtailed. In Orange, residents were emotionally and behaviourally disturbed, preferring their own world to that of a group. They played separately and only interacted when involved in a fight.

In contrast, the strong child cultures in Cyan clearly affected residents' behaviour. They spent the majority of their time together and were rarely allowed to be alone. When a member of staff was about to leave, the children would spend much time discussing its likely impact on the group. Plans were formulated to say goodbye and to vet potential replacements. Children were encouraged to view the event as a loss and to discuss their feelings.

This method of analysis found staff cultures to be more prevalent than child cultures. However, as will be seen, both have the potential to support or undermine the quality of care in a home. The following table summarises the findings.

## Structure and culture

The previous chapter concluded with three possible patterns of relationships between the three types of goal that constitute the structure of a home. In the first group, societal, formal and belief goals were concordant and where this occurred, homes were forward looking. In the second, there was some discord or at least ambiguity between the goals and the consequences were fluctuating fortunes for the home. Finally, there were two homes in which societal, formal and belief goals were entirely discordant and there was consistent deterioration in the situation over the 12 months of fieldwork.

Table 7.1: The strength of staff and child cultures in the nine homes

| Homes | Strength of culture | |
| | Staff Culture | Child Culture |
| --- | --- | --- |
| Blue | Medium | Weak |
| Yellow | Strong | Weak |
| Green | Medium | Medium |
| Red | Strong | Strong |
| Magenta | Weak | Weak |
| Orange | Medium | Weak |
| Cyan | Strong | Strong |
| Indigo | Strong | Medium |
| White | Strong | Strong |

The results on which this table is based can be found in Appendix Three.

In this chapter, evidence on the prevailing cultures in the homes has been presented. It is now possible to explore whether there is a link between structure and culture. It was not assumed at the outset that there was. Cultures are not necessarily positive and it may have been the case that homes with a discordant culture produced a group response from children and staff as much as homes with a positive culture. Several relationships between structures and cultures were possible, but it was found that four were most likely to occur.

First is a situation where there are high levels of structural concordance which cause a healthy staff culture which supports the aims and objectives of the residential centre and maintains a strong or fragmented child culture. Second is a home where some discord between the formal, belief goals and societal goals produces a strong staff culture which frequently challenges and occasionally undermines the aims and objectives of management. Here, a child culture is likely to be limited. Third, is a highly discordant structure which causes the staff culture to be strong and counterproductive to what is being attempted on behalf of children. Fourth is where the discordant structure means that staff cultures are weak. In these last two scenarios, there are likely to be times when the child culture challenges and undermines staff.

*(1) Concordant structure leads to healthy culture*

In Cyan, Red and Yellow, concordance was found between the societal, formal and belief goals. In all three, there was also evidence of strong staff cultures. Indeed, the staff groups responded to tasks and events in such a way that structures were enhanced. For example when a child refused to go to school at Cyan, since it was part of a wider therapeutic community with a school on site, a coherent response was practically guaranteed. The staff group were clear and consistent; it was regarded as a privilege to be able to attend school. Those refusing to go stayed behind in the living unit dressed in school uniform to get on quietly with work set by teachers under the staff's supervision. Seeing the other children being allowed the 'privilege' of going off to school every morning and being in the minority staying back was usually an incentive to return to class.

In Cyan the staff actively sought both to encourage and control the child culture. The whole 'group', children and staff, came together for regular meetings to discuss a wide range of issues, from daily routines to a child's needs. Superficially, at least, decisions were shared, although it was the adults who had the final say. There were short periods during the study when Cyan came under severe stress. At those times, an almost constant series of meetings would occur with staff being made accountable for their mistakes and children being held responsible for their behaviour and being reminded of the goals of the home (and, *de facto*, why they were there).

At Yellow, the home offering respite care, staff responses to a parent's visit were well rehearsed. Parents came in and out every day, sometimes unexpectedly, even when their children were not staying. Staff were used to giving their time to families and had informally allocated a room for private discussions with parents in difficulty. Staff made it clear to new recruits that their task was a partnership with the child's family. Unsurprisingly, parents viewed Yellow as a source of support and some formed friendships with staff. The goals of this home were manifest in the dialogue between staff and in their interaction with children and families.

At Red, the easy manner in which staff dealt with a young person who had to be restrained demonstrated a cohesive staff culture. Staff spent considerable time with residents so warning signs of unresolved disputes and tensions that might require restraint were anticipated. The staff worked together to stop problems escalating, discussing informally how each might defuse potential explosions; considering the age and circumstances of residents, restraint incidents were few. For example, young people would be separated into different parts of the house, diverted or provided with opportunities to discuss problems. Typically, humour was used to reduce tensions. If restraint became necessary, most staff coped efficiently.

These were the three homes in this category where concordance between structural goals had led to a healthy staff culture. In two of them, Cyan and Red, the child culture was also strong and generally supported the aims and objectives of the home. In Yellow, the respite home with many children coming and going each day, the child culture was weak. Nothing in children's actions, however, undermined the running of the home.

*(2) Some discord in structure produces some problems in culture*

Four of the homes fell between the two extremes of structural concordance and discord; White, Blue, Green and Magenta. In the first three, some discord and ambiguity in the structures tended to be mirrored by the mixed nature of staff group responses. At Green at the beginning of the study, for example, the three staff teams that covered the rota acted almost as separate entities. Asking members of the same team what would happen if a child stole from a fellow resident or fell ill, a clear cultural pattern emerged; but within each group different answers were given by different teams. Moreover, some were actively undermining the goals of the home. Referred to by the new manager coming to Green during the study year as 'good', 'medium' and 'poor', these three staff teams gave mixed messages to the children.

At Blue, as Chapter Four explains, a new statement of purpose and function was viewed as a mixed blessing by a previously cohesive staff group. In a situation where staff were faced with increasing numbers of adolescents admitted in an emergency rather than the younger children who were intended to stay long periods of time, tasks such as 'a new child arrives' were met with different reactions. Some staff felt comfortable with the prospect of 'stroppy' adolescents but others withdrew and focused their attention on the remaining children from the existing group with whom they were familiar. Staff group responses worked against each other and the new structure of the home faltered. However, the training introduced by the new managers had some effects; it gave staff lacking confidence the skills to work with young people and it brought staff together again thus achieving a more consistent response.

At White, a staff culture helped to prop up a faltering structure. The small staff team had worked together for many years and had built up what they called the 'fed and bed' culture, with a focus on providing food, shelter and a warm living environment. The arrival of a new manager threatened this order but, in the event, he took the option of fitting in with the existing approach rather than seeking to modify it.

The child culture at White was particularly strong in some areas but weak in others. Mealtimes certainly appeared to have a common social order. The dining room was set with two large tables. There was no rigid seating plan but girls tended to sit at one table and boys at the other, each table having one staff member to supervise. There was a pecking order that permitted the eldest resident to sit nearest to staff. Conversations were animated and wide ranging and seldom involved any disputes. But while meal times had a civilising influence on the home, there did not appear to be much social cohesion among residents when it came to questions of family and social relationships or attention to health needs.

Child cultures at Green were also of varying strength. Only children stealing from each other produced a strong response. Most of the children had been victims of sexual abuse and there was a normative emphasis, encouraged by staff, upon respecting each other's privacy. Consequently, theft assumed greater significance than it might in other places. Offenders were heavily censured and isolated from a group usually united in its support for the victim.

At Blue, the child culture was sporadic at most times excepting the group holiday. Ordinarily, the young people lived their own separate lives with their own activities and interests. In two caravans on a beach holiday camp site, proximity and surroundings produced, momentarily, a common identity. The holiday atmosphere allowed them to extend curfews, push out boundaries and relax other rules. The change was brief. On their return, the old ways emerged but the holiday served as a reminder of how the group could cohere and interact. It was referred to with affection and the next holiday eagerly awaited.

The pattern of discord found in the structural goals of White, Blue and Green seems to be reflected in the mixed pattern of cultural responses of children and staff. At Magenta, however, whose idiosyncrasies were discussed in the previous chapter, the cultural responses of both staff and children were weak; and, where they did exist, were almost always negative. Magenta, therefore, defies the hypothesis suggested in the opening pages of this chapter. Indeed, in other respects also, it is an 'outlier', as will be discussed in future chapters.

*(3) Highly discordant structure causes staff culture to be strong but counter-productive*

High levels of discord were evident between the structural goals of Indigo and Orange. In Indigo there was evidence of a staff culture but it tended to undermine the structure of the home. Staff culture actively worked against key principles of the *Children Act*, 1989, did not support the formal aims and objectives of the home and shared the manager's disillusionment and lack of belief in what could be achieved.

This pattern can be illustrated in the response of staff to successive residents coming to court to be sentenced for burglaries. The court appearance was treated solely as a transport task, getting the young person to and from court. The interaction between staff and residents could not be distinguished from that between staff and other offenders awaiting their fate. There was no sense of accountability and no plans to prepare for the various decisions a magistrate could make. Nothing in the trips to court would indicate to a young person that this was an unhappy situation.

Had there been one or two dissidents among a generally negative crew, the home might have had something to commend it. Unfortunately, the apathy with which visits to court were treated was echoed in other contexts of the staff world as it related to the children. Going to school, keeping in touch with relatives, getting in on time, going to bed at a reasonable hour (and getting up), watching appropriate television programmes; all of these supervision and care tasks were treated by staff with the same easy come, easy go attitude that would have horrified even the most errant of parents whom residents had left behind. Needless to say, the situation was severely exacerbated by the child culture at Indigo which, as has been seen in several examples, was almost entirely negative.

*(4) Highly discordant structure leads to weak staff culture and no child culture*

Eight of the nine homes have now been discussed. At the last, Orange, a discordant structure was associated with a staff culture of medium strength, which, where it did exist, undermined the formal goals of the home; in addition, there was apparently no child culture to speak of.

The staff group failed to cohere when the children were abusive. An episode with one small boy, Darren, serves as a good example. He got angry when asked to get his dirty washing from his room. He swore at a senior member of staff calling her a 'fat bitch' which she accepted without murmur or reprimand. Half an hour later, Darren got worked up again when asked by a second member of staff to turn off the television and to read quietly to himself. He called her a 'miserable bitch' to which she shouted back, 'get up to your room or you'll find out how miserable I am.' Some staff ignored Darren altogether, some walked away or even laughed. One or two inconsistencies like this do not necessarily indicate a difficulty, but in combination, over many areas of a child's life and over an extended period of time, the quality of life inside a home begins to suffer.

The lack of cultural response was also manifest when two Orange staff began a relationship. Some staff felt it was immoral, others that it was none of their business. Some were so eager to be involved they used it as an opportunity to talk to the children about relationships. At no time did the staff group discuss together what should be done. The matter came to a head when marriage was suggested. The manager moved one member of staff to a nearby unit and the other went on extended sick leave. The children, needless to say, thought the staff had left because they had been naughty.

Orange cared for mainly younger children who stayed for long periods of time. Yet there was no obvious culture among the resident group. They were fragmented on nearly all the dimensions where the research looked for a common purpose. At the outset, a fragmented child culture was said to be no bad thing. But in the context of a home with a confused set of aims and objectives and a group of staff who seldom find consistency of approach, the result is rather depressing. The children were in the home but they could hardly be said to live there. One could not say that they suffered by being at Orange but it appeared to be a less than beneficial experience.

Table 7.2: The strength of staff and child cultures in the nine homes and the support offered to the homes' goals

| Homes | Strength and direction of culture | |
| | Staff Culture | Child Culture |
| --- | --- | --- |
| Blue | Medium, neither | Weak, neither |
| Yellow | Strong, positive | Weak, positive |
| Green | Medium, neither | Medium, neither |
| Red | Strong, positive | Strong, positive |
| Magenta | Weak, negative | Weak, negative |
| Orange | Medium, negative | Weak, negative |
| Cyan | Strong, positive | Strong, positive |
| Indigo | Strong, negative | Medium, negative |
| White | Strong, positive | Strong, neither |

The full results on which this table is based can be found in Appendix Three.

## Summary

The previous discussion demonstrates two important findings. First, it is important that cultures among staff and children should be strong, but just as important that they should support the aims and objectives of the home. The pattern shown in Table 7.2 emerged in respect to this question.

Second, the findings indicate differences in the concordance between structural goals, staff cultures and child cultures. There are numerous possible relationships between but four common patterns were found. Moreover, with the exception of Magenta, the cultures in the homes were more or less as might have been predicted, given their structure. So:

- where there was a concordant structure (in Cyan, Red and Yellow), a strong and supportive staff culture and a supportive or fragmented child culture was found.
- where there was some discord in the structure (in White, Blue and Green, but not Magenta), staff cultures were of medium strength or strong and a mixed blessing to the manager. The child cultures also varied in their strength and usefulness to the running of the home.

Magenta behaved in an unexpected way, in that some discord between its structural goals led staff and child cultures to be weak.

- where there was considerable discord between the societal, formal and belief goals of a home, the staff and child cultures were either medium or strong but counter-productive, as in Indigo, or led to an absence of child culture, as in Orange.

## Other influences upon child cultures

In addition to structures or staff cultures, there may be other influences upon the children's world, for example their age and the length of time they have lived together and the varying needs of all those brought under one roof. The steady stream of children arriving and departing is now a seemingly omnipresent feature of residential life and staff and children have developed cultures to cope. In some homes, for instance Red and Magenta, the turnover of children was so high that the roll call was completely different by the end of the study from that recorded at the beginning.

The difficulties that can occur are illustrated by the case of Gina who arrived at Magenta at the start of the study period. Her mother and social worker left Gina to sit with her collection of carrier bags in the kitchen, protesting that she was being allocated to the wrong part of the campus. It had been agreed that she should go to a small satellite unit as she was unlikely to cope with living in a large group. But the staff decided otherwise and Gina was placed in a unit that was ill-prepared to meet her needs. Staff struggled to make a meaningful relationship with her but she left for home after three months of upheaval.

Gina's behaviour had a deleterious effect on the rest of the group. Running away increased as did violence towards new arrivals. One such attack by the two girls who had been at the home the longest shocked staff with its ferocity. The home suspended the new girl and not the established members, thus making it difficult for any newcomer to join the group. Their culture excluded outsiders. One badly managed arrival seemed to set the entire establishment back several months.

Despite difficulties associated with arrival and departure, there was little evidence that the mix of children in homes affected either the development or nature of child cultures. There may be occasions when mixing children with widely different needs together is, to say the least, unhelpful. At Red, the mix of children was considerable, yet there were still strong and positive child cultures therein. The age of children might also be expected to affect the ability of the children to form group cultures. Orange, the youngest child group, did indeed produce one of the weakest child cultures whereas, as just described, the home with the oldest residents, Red, had one of the strongest. But the other six homes, which provided care for 13 to 16 years olds, displayed a range of cultures - strong and weak, concordant and discordant.

Overall, outside influences, such as the mix of children within a home, the age and characteristics of the child group and the length of time they live together were found to have less effect upon the child cultures than expected. Cultures flourished in seemingly adverse conditions such as at Red and Cyan. The evidence suggests that, rather than being shaped by external forces, there was a linear relationship between structure, staff culture and child culture. A concordant structure produced the strongest and most accordant staff cultures. In turn, these adult cultures promoted the most concordant and positive child cultures.

## Conclusion

There appears to be a relationship between patterns of structure in children's homes and the cultural response of staff and children. Indeed, the concordance between societal, formal and belief goals is a good predictor of the strength of staff culture and the support which that culture will bring to the aims and objectives of a home. Only Magenta behaved unexpectedly, with a reasonable degree of concordance between the goals of the home seemingly having little effect on how the staff responded to different tasks and situations.

The model has been useful in understanding the strength and orientation of child cultures but of less value in predicting them. At the extremities, that is where there was high goal concordance and strong supportive staff cultures, or where there was high discordance and weak staff cultures, the response of children fulfilled research expectations. In between, the picture is hazy. Why should this be the case?

With children and young people, the relationship with the home is different from that enjoyed by the staff. They are not paid to be there. They are not subject to the same conditions if they transgress rules.

There is no Volume Four of guidance for children. Even if they enjoy living in a children's home and sense the benefits it brings in terms of their safety, development or reduction of anxiety, children mostly do not want to be there. Much better to be like the other pupils in school, complaining about parents but nonetheless being able to live with them.

Is the presence of a child culture important? Much literature on residential care has stressed the need to fragment the child world. This is now shown to be an exaggeration, perhaps appropriate to larger establishments such as boarding schools or secure units. In two of the three children's homes with concordant goals and a positive staff culture, the child culture was also strong. What is more, it further supported the aims and objectives of the home. In Yellow, the rapid turnover of children coming for respite meant that the child world would always be fragmented. What is important is that children implicitly understand the goals of residential care for those looked after, that they comprehend the formal interpretation of this in the place in which they live and that they see a manager who believes that he or she can achieve something on their behalf. The resident culture must not have an opportunity to cohere against these goals of residence, not at any point in a home's development, for it is clear from charting change over the year that cultures can outstay the residents in the home. The events at Indigo - Gary disrupting mealtimes; staff barricaded into the office; televisions being sold for drugs - will be remembered for some time. Late attention to the societal, formal and belief goals will help, but remedial effects will not be immediate. What is described instrumentally here comes to hover like a cloud above the children's home so that even the most cheery and optimistic of entrants rapidly becomes depressed.

These effects are manifest in the holiday taken by Blue. In a new context rules were reviewed. Staff reconsidered their relationships with residents who, in turn, reflected on their relationship with one other. Given that the weather was dreadful and the caravan in which staff and children stayed was of much poorer quality than the children's home, it was more the change of context than the context itself that created a temporary improvement in the culture of the home. Unfortunately, cultural difficulties that occurred several months, occasionally several years, ago become embedded in the fabric of some children's homes.

The relationship identified in this research is linear; structural goals influence staff culture, which affects child culture which, in combination, determine outcomes of homes. The relationship has been established, but could the direction be reversed? Can the child culture determine the structure of homes? The evidence from Red would seem to refute this possibility. Adolescents, kicked out of home and failing in a variety of foster and residential contexts are hardly promising candidates to fill an inner-city children's home. Yet Red achieved its goals. The comparison between Orange and Cyan which effectively had similar clientele and functions is also revealing on this point. The former had more stable premises, more resources and residents who were relatively quiescent compared with the latter. Yet, without prejudicing the results described in the following chapter, it was Cyan that succeeded in its task.

Maybe the relationship between structure and culture can be explained in other ways. Could it be the leader who is most significant? Red did not have a manager for some of the time and, while the leaders of Cyan and Yellow were extremely efficient, they were not insightful charismatics. In children's homes, the key is not who leads but what the leadership is intended to convey. If the intention is to set a residential context apart from much else in society, to sit at the radical end of practice, a charismatic maverick will excite. But the results of this research would suggest that for children's homes it is the manager's understanding of societal and formal goals with a belief in what can be achieved, given the children's needs and the resources available, that sets the tone.

Finally, how would these results look in completely different contexts? Can they be used to explain why one hotel in a chain aiming for a consistent service is better than another? This is beyond the Unit's sphere of expertise, except that another part of the Dartington Trust is a conference centre set in the mediaeval courtyard of the estate. Originally its role was unclear; at best it was conceived of as a money spinner to support other parts of the charitable enterprise. For many years it struggled with staff problems, variable standards of services but, by the standards of consumer evaluation, good outcomes. More importantly, despite an unparalleled setting, high prices and extremely good food it consistently lost money. But since it has been agreed by the Charity Commission, the estate trustees and the local manager that the goal of the conference centre should be to provide a context in which people could be exposed to new ideas and so to acknowledge that this may not be sufficient to balance the financial books, it has run without any of the problems that beset it at the outset. Societal, formal and belief goals have come into accord.

What about other public sector settings? A local authority social services department is difficult to equate since it seldom has children in sufficient numbers to allow a culture to exist, except in residential care. Education is rather different and from reading seminal texts, such as Rutter and colleagues' *15,000 Hours*, or talking to head teachers or chief education officers, it would seem that the ideas developed in this study do translate. The societal goals for schools have a much longer pedigree than those fashioned for children's homes. But confusion over what schools are meant to do - to educate in the widest sense, exercise control or achieve in pupils an agreed level of competency - can undermine a school and a headteacher's belief in the job; these confusions can be felt in the cultures of schools as much as they are described in children's homes in the preceding pages.

So much for culture, what about outcome? It is to this question that the study now turns.

# 8 Structure, cultures and outcome for the homes

Child care researchers have become used to identifying and sometimes explaining outcomes for individual children. But what about outcomes for a residential unit? All nine homes continued to function throughout the period of the study, which, by the reckoning of some managers, might be considered a good result. For operators of a private home, remaining in profit is certainly viewed positively, whereas, in therapeutic communities, belief usually remains unshaken despite recurring financial crises. Some long-term homes consider keeping hold of the young person to be beneficial, in contrast to Yellow, which viewed the return home of children to be a prerequisite of a good outcome This chapter is concerned with what makes a children's home good or bad.

Many experienced in the ways of residential care might feel able to make such judgements within minutes of entering a children's home; using the smell and feel of institutions mentioned in Chapter Four. But first impressions can be misleading. The naval officer boarding a ship glances at the state of the gangway, the smartness of the sentry and the alertness of the crew. This tells him or her a lot about the mood of the ship's company, but he or she also knows that such indicators will mean little if the engine is not working. Others use the performance indicators of organisation and management analysts to make a judgement, but Auschwitz and Dachau were run with a ruthless efficiency. Most observers have tired of charismatic, innovative leaders who fan excitement in visitors and create an illusion of a good home; the unmasking of Beck in Leicestershire and the Pindown experiment in Staffordshire has put paid to that.

Over a period of at least a year, each of the nine homes was visited many times, including two three day stays and many other contacts such as letter, telephone and facsimile communications with both residents and staff. There were a multitude of factors which appeared to indicate that a home was well run, a nice place in which to live in and liked by staff and residents. The researchers visiting each home made judgements independent of each other to check whether each was drawing the same conclusions from the same evidence. It was obvious from this exercise, as it will have become obvious to the reader, that some homes were better than others.

The extent to which others find the assessment contained in this chapter reliable will reflect their view on the indicators selected. If a high rate of running away from a home sheltering children under 12 years of age is not a cause of concern to the reader, then this chapter is unlikely to be helpful. If a failure to consider the principles of the *Children Act*, 1989 does not engender dismay, then the following pages are unlikely to excite. Or if the openness of residential homes to *bona fide* visitors is of little interest, then the observations outlined here will mean little.

Part of this analysis involved abandoning factors not found to correlate with the quality of a home. It is disappointing to report that training of staff does not indicate a good residential centre for children looked after, but as so few (8%) had relevant qualifications, linking the numbers of qualified staff to outcomes was not possible. When other relevant training is considered - such as nursing, teacher training or counselling - or work experience - say in hospitals, schools or youth work - the factor was similarly unhelpful because it was not possible to generalise from the experience of a few individuals. Economic indicators of demand and supply also counted for little because even the most inadequate home was nearly always full. Unfortunately, faced with a difficult case under conditions of duress, social workers continue to look for a bed first and worry about the quality of placement second.

None of this scrutiny of outcomes for homes would count for much if those found to be good did not achieve beneficial outcomes for the child. But it was important to come to an understanding of outcomes for homes first, because this would provide some validation of the work reported in previous chapters on structure and culture in homes. In short, is a children's home with concordant structural goals (which is now known to lead to a strong and supportive staff culture with a complementary or fragmented child culture) a 'good home'? There is a danger of creating a tautology in answering this question. To say that a home operates in relation to the *Children Act*, 1989 and Volume Four of the guidance or that it has clear aims and objectives is almost the same as saying societal and formal goals - described in Chapter Six - coincide. But taking several outcome indicators in combination is sufficient to avoid this trap.

From the methods described in Chapter Three, some 43 indicators of a home's performance were collected. Simple correlation and ranking exercises found 20 factors were indicative of a 'good home', of which 12 in combination appeared to produce the best fit. These variables can be classified under three headings:

- how staff, children and visitors perceive the children's home,

- how staff and children are observed to behave in the home, and

- how good was the practice in the home in relation to contemporary standards, including the principles which underpin the *Children Act*, 1989.

It may help the reader to know that the some of the outcome factors selected for this study overlap with those explored by Sinclair and Gibbs whose project was taking place simultaneously.

## How staff, children and other visitors perceive the home

The difficulty of ascertaining children's perspectives on their placements has been touched on in previous chapters. Nevertheless, a reasonably accurate picture was assembled on whether children felt cared for and safe in their placement, not only by asking them directly but also by observing them in their interactions with staff. If they sought staff company and this was reciprocated then a reasonably supportive environment was assumed to exist. In Indigo, staff appeared to have limited interest in spending time with the children and, consequently, young people's behaviour could be attention seeking and disruptive. Individual and group conversations held with children and the diaries written by a number of residents spoke volumes about the nature of the interventions. Natasha at Cyan wrote:

> I have been here for nearly two years and I've enjoyed it. The adults in Cyan are very understanding, they have a feeling about

how we are... Later on most of us are going to talking time where we can speak about our problems and also things we find hard to talk about, but sometimes it is helpful to have meetings and talking time.

In contrast, children in other homes appeared to crave individual attention from staff. In Orange, for example, one boy wrote about spending all afternoon waiting for one of the members of staff to fulfil a promise to spend some time with him. Another child from the same home measured the quality of her day against the criterion of one member of staff being on shift.

The qualitative nature of children's feelings makes the interpretation of findings difficult. However, in four homes (Cyan, Yellow, Red and White) it was clear through the consistency of the children's responses and from observations of their interactions with the staff that they all felt cared for. In three homes (Blue, Green, Magenta) the picture was mixed, with some children feeling insecure and fighting for staff attention. It has been noted that in Indigo, the situation was consistently poor.

A second measure of a 'good home' was the warmth of welcome extended to visitors, particularly family members or friends of the children but also to researchers. In four of the nine homes, staff talked openly and with enthusiasm about their work and were prepared to make time to show visitors around. In another four, by contrast, parents were viewed as an irritation. Nadine joined Orange half way through the study. Her parents were not invited; she was sent to what was called 'Jane's old room'; and her anxiety about having the right school uniform for the following day took several hours to be resolved. The frequency of parental visits and of children returning to see their temporary 'home' are good indicators of the warmth of residential centres.

Most residential centres believe they shelter extremely difficult and disturbed youngsters. Set against the relative calm of family life, their observations are probably correct. A different perspective, however, comes from asking children whether or not the other residents behave reasonably. Naturally, a 16 year old kicked out of home has different standards from those of the clinical psychiatrist. Indeed, in six of the homes, residents were satisfied that the behaviour of their peers was reasonable, even though this included considerable disruption. Only in

Indigo, where it will be recalled that one resident terrorised the others, was there total dissatisfaction on this issue.

One adolescent at Red explains how misbehaviour is not something necessarily to be applauded by other residents:

> New kids come in and, at the start, they try and take the piss. They might bring a bit of dope in or stay out late without telling anyone what they are doing. And that's hassle for the staff but it's also hassle for us. It means somebody has to be checking up, keeping an eye on what we have in our rooms or 'phoning around to see who's where when they might be doing something with us. So the new ones have to learn that we don't do what we did in other children's homes. That Red's not like that. Not for them, not for the staff, not for us.

Finally, in respect to perceptions, much has been said in this study about the manager's belief in his or her work, what about the staff themselves? If asked why they were working in the home, did staff talk about the needs of children or did they refer to the absence of anything better to do? The picture was mixed and, naturally, reflected the fortunes of the home at different stages during the fieldwork and the complement of workers employed at successive moments. Again, in four of the homes the results were positive in that staff clearly had pride in their work but in two, Orange and Indigo, there was consistent apathy.

At Green, staff attitudes to visitors came to influence the children's perceptions, as the following quotations indicate:

> Staff member: we get all kinds coming in here looking around. Social workers, inspectors, you researchers, even the family members want to come. We've got a job to do. That's what people don't understand. But you have to put up with them. In and out they go. Half the time we don't know who they are.

> Child: we're a bit cut off I suppose. There's a lot of people coming to see us but I don't know who they are or what they do. And we don't seem to go anywhere. You notice it when my mum comes. There's nowhere really for us to go. So you end up hanging around like a spare part or we go out to the shops or something.

These results of the analysis of the perceptions of staff, children and visitors are summarised in the next table. A score of two is given if the factor applies, one if it applied some of the time over the 12 months of scrutiny and zero if it did not apply at all. In the long run, when researchers have digested the result, and applied the factors to other homes, some form of weighting of the factors can be undertaken as it is highly probable that one or two have more predictive power than the others. For now, a simple addition is sufficient.

## The behaviour of staff and children in the home

It is an old psychological adage that what people say is not necessarily the same as what they do. It is noticeable in the research that the evidence on staff and children's behaviour was consistently less optimistic than that on staff and children's perceptions of the situation. For example, despite four of the homes having staff who had pride in the job, only Yellow and Cyan employed people who were aspirant, both for themselves and the children, and confident in addressing the needs of the children. This gap between rhetoric and reality has beset residential care for many years.

Table 8.1: How staff, children and other visitors perceive the home

| | The Nine Homes | | | | | | | | | |
|---|---|---|---|---|---|---|---|---|---|---|
| Outcomes | B | Y | G | R | M | O | C | I | W | Total |
| Child feels cared for | - | ✓ | - | ✓ | - | - | ✓ | x | ✓ | 12 |
| Warm and friendly | - | ✓ | - | ✓ | - | x | ✓ | x | - | 10 |
| Children like visitors | ✓ | ✓ | ✓ | ✓ | - | - | ✓ | x | ✓ | 14 |
| Staff have pride | - | ✓ | - | ✓ | - | x | ✓ | x | ✓ | 11 |
| Total | 5 | 8 | 5 | 8 | 4 | 2 | 8 | 0 | 7 | 47 |

Key:✓=2; -=1; x=0

Levels of sickness can be a useful barometer of staff satisfaction. In Orange and Indigo, levels were much higher than in the other homes, reflecting the size of the staff group - small groups having less cover within the teams - and the availability of relief staff. In Orange sickness levels among the large staff group were extremely high until budget cuts made the availability of relief scarce (even then it remained relatively high). In Cyan, which had the lowest staff to child ratio, sickness levels were at their lowest and, probably unwisely, staff regularly turned up for work when quite unwell. It has been reported that one of the consequences of such commitment was a high turnover as staff simply burned out.

An indication of satisfaction for children is running away. Such behaviour has to be seen in a context; breaking out of a maximum security prison must be viewed with greater alarm than a child failing to turn up for respite care or an adolescent staying away from his 'independent' bedsit all night. In Red and Cyan rates of running away were lower than had been expected, especially at Red where half of the residents arrived with a long history of running away but did not do so again.

The young people at Red said they had no wish, no need to run away. If they wanted to leave, of course, then the staff would not oppose their wishes, even if it was thought inadvisable. The door was left ajar for people to return if their plans fell through. The decision to stay or go belonged to the young person and, in this context, running away was neither a realistic proposition nor a word in the residents' vocabulary.

The use of space in the home by staff and residents also came to be recognised as a useful outcome indicator. Like a family home, a residential centre should be more than a place to sleep. Even hotels which accommodate total strangers have arrangements for guests to meet socially. Of course a 16 year old wishing to protect his girlfriend from the gaze of parents by sitting her before the television and not around the dinner table is not a cause for alarm. But some social niceties would be expected, even for the most awkward of teenagers. Noting who talks to whom, where and what about is not only interesting, it suggests to the observer how well a home is working.

Mealtimes are important in this respect. It was reported in Chapter Four that staff and children in Indigo became fearful of eating with Gary, a resident who had become uncontrollable. Several months after Gary's departure, children were still turning up late for meals, grabbing a sandwich and eating in groups of two or three around the house, normally in front of a television or computer game. Identifying the focal point of a home can also help understand its quality. If it is the kitchen or dining room, a full social life involving all those living and working in the home as possible. If it is the television room, then Chris Evans and the cast of *Neighbours* will probably have as much call on children's attention as the manager or staff. If it is the 'office' as at Orange, Indigo and Magenta, then the child's world will probably be separated from the staff world.

The separation between staff and residents that can emerge is evident in the following quotation from an interview with Gavin who talked about a rumpus following a television set being stolen at Indigo:

> First thing today we got up and a telly's gone. And nobody's broken in. And then they find out that Shane isn't in his room. So they (the staff) all disappear off to the office to decide what to do. We (the children) were all in the kitchen having a laugh. Then Shane comes back about 11 and he's high as a kite and somebody comes out the office to ask him about the telly. And Shane tells them to f*** off, he's innocent and there's a bit of pushing and shoving when drugs are mentioned. And we all start joining in and it ends up with them lot (the staff) in the office and us lot outside banging on the door, calling them all kinds and in the end they were so scared they called the police.

These findings on staff and children's behaviour in the home are summarised in the following table. Again, there is considerable variation between the homes.

Table 8.2: The behaviour of staff and children in the home

| Outcomes | The Nine Homes | | | | | | | | | |
|---|---|---|---|---|---|---|---|---|---|---|
| | B | Y | G | R | M | O | C | I | W | Total |
| Staff aspirant | x | ✓ | x | - | x | x | ✓ | x | x | 5 |
| Low sick rate | - | ✓ | - | ✓ | ✓ | x | ✓ | x | ✓ | 12 |
| Low absconding | - | ✓ | - | ✓ | x | x | ✓ | x | ✓ | 10 |
| Effective space use | - | ✓ | - | ✓ | x | x | ✓ | x | ✓ | 10 |
| Total | 3 | 8 | 3 | 7 | 2 | 0 | 8 | 0 | 6 | 37 |

## Quality of practice in relation to contemporary standards

When the philanthropists, Dr. Guthrie, Josiah Mason and William Muller founded their institutions, they acted, as they thought, in the best interests of the children. But 20 or 30 to a dormitory is not acceptable in a world where aims and objectives stressing the need to respect each child's individuality and to work in partnership with young people and their families have become an expectation even if not, unfortunately, the norm. Some of these indicators have been covered in the chapter on structure, but here the focus is much more specific; does the home have something that resembles a statement of purpose and function? Are there care plans for each child? Is there a mechanism for listening to people working and living in the home? And how does the manager link with other parts of the personal social services world?

Five of the nine homes had clear aims and objectives written down in a policy statement. Orange and Indigo had a statement of purpose which manager and staff had concluded no longer matched the service being provided. Evidence on objectives for individual residents was even more disquieting. All the children had some sort of social work plan but only 28% had a care plan drawn up by the home at a review involving the child, his or her family and the field social worker. Small wonder that children continue to experience institutional neglect or that issues of control overwhelm child care aims, such as to foster better relations with relatives, get the child to school or into work and promote psychological and physical health.

In only two of the homes, Yellow and Cyan, was the manager aware of and integrated with the wider child care world. Both of these homes were run by voluntary organisations, making interaction with the purchasing divisions of the local authority not only more difficult but also a necessity. Most of the local authority homes remained reluctant to look to the world outside and were even critical of the social services department that fed them.

At White, for example, the manager considered what he called the 'care system' to be a

> bit of a con. What do children's homes do that parents can't? All these kids should be back with their relatives and they should be given the money we use to keep places like this going.

Had this manager talked to parents or visited their homes, had he been aware of relevant research or participated in local authority case reviews which considered the contribution of residence in the context of children's care plans (and invariably indicated a reunion in the near future), the shallowness of his statement would have been understood. As it was, White remained rather isolated from the outside world.

The findings on quality of practice in the homes are summarised in the following table.

Table 8.3: Quality of practice in relation to contemporary standards

| Outcomes | The Nine Homes | | | | | | | | | |
|---|---|---|---|---|---|---|---|---|---|---|
| | B | Y | G | R | M | O | C | I | W | Total |
| Care Plans | - | ✓ | - | - | - | x | ✓ | x | - | 9 |
| Manager & context | - | ✓ | - | - | x | - | ✓ | - | x | 9 |
| Residents have say | - | ✓ | - | ✓ | x | x | ✓ | x | - | 9 |
| Staff have say | - | ✓ | - | ✓ | x | x | ✓ | x | ✓ | 10 |
| Total | 4 | 8 | 4 | 6 | 1 | 1 | 8 | 1 | 4 | 37 |

## Structure, culture and outcome

There are dozens of factors which might be used as an indicator of quality in children's homes. The 12 selected for the preceding analysis were, in combination, reasonably robust in picking out the good from the poor home, in that they have stood up to a number of cross checks between the researchers and between research and practitioners. The prospective testing of the practice tools which has emerged from the study will be needed to satisfy the keen scientist, but as a measure of outcome the 12 factors are sufficient.

The following table summarises the results in the three outcome areas for each of the nine homes. Clearly, Yellow, Red and Cyan stand out from White, Blue and Green which, in turn, all emerge from their exercise with better reputations than Magenta, Orange or Indigo.

Table 8.4: Structure, culture and outcome: results for each home

| Outcomes | The Nine Homes | | | | | | | | | |
|---|---|---|---|---|---|---|---|---|---|---|
| | Good homes | | | Medium homes | | | Poor homes | | | |
| | Y | R | C | B | G | W | M | O | I | Total |
| Child feels cared for | ✓ | ✓ | ✓ | - | - | ✓ | - | - | x | 12 |
| Warm and friendly | ✓ | ✓ | ✓ | - | - | - | - | x | x | 10 |
| Children like visitors | ✓ | ✓ | ✓ | ✓ | ✓ | ✓ | - | - | x | 14 |
| Staff have pride | ✓ | ✓ | ✓ | - | - | ✓ | - | x | x | 11 |
| Staff aspirant | ✓ | - | ✓ | x | x | x | x | x | x | 5 |
| Low sick rate | ✓ | ✓ | ✓ | - | - | ✓ | ✓ | x | x | 12 |
| Low absconding | ✓ | ✓ | ✓ | - | - | ✓ | x | x | x | 10 |
| Effective space use | ✓ | ✓ | ✓ | - | - | ✓ | x | x | x | 10 |
| Care Plans | ✓ | - | ✓ | - | - | - | - | x | x | 9 |
| Manager & context | ✓ | - | ✓ | - | - | x | x | - | - | 9 |
| Residents have say | ✓ | ✓ | ✓ | - | - | - | x | x | x | 9 |
| Staff have say | ✓ | ✓ | ✓ | - | - | ✓ | x | x | x | 10 |
| Total | 24 | 21 | 24 | 12 | 12 | 17 | 7 | 3 | 1 | 121 |

The question that remains is whether the quality of children's homes as measured by the above method is any way related to structure and culture of the homes as explained in Chapters Six and Seven? The hypothesis outlined at the beginning of the study might be recalled, namely that

- a children's home with concordant societal, formal and belief goals (that is to say a healthy structure) will produce

- a strong staff culture which supports the aims and objectives of the home, and

- either a strong child culture which also supports the formal goals of the residential centre or a fragmented child culture that does not undermine it.

Table 8.5: Structure, culture and outcome: a summary by home

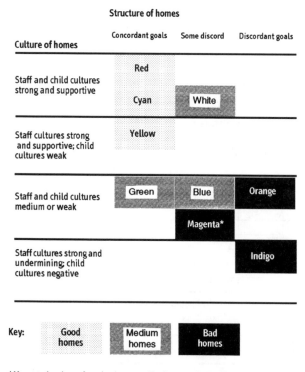

Structure of homes

| Culture of homes | Concordant goals | Some discord | Discordant goals |
|---|---|---|---|
| Staff and child cultures strong and supportive | Red<br>Cyan | White | |
| Staff cultures strong and supportive; child cultures weak | Yellow | | |
| Staff and child cultures medium or weak | Green | Blue<br>Magenta* | Orange |
| Staff cultures strong and undermining; child cultures negative | | | Indigo |

Key: Good homes | Medium homes | Bad homes

*Magenta has been found to be an outlier in several chapters

It was secondly hypothesised that if these conditions applied, the children's home will be of a high quality or defined (using the criteria of this or Sinclair and Gibb's study) as a 'good home'. The table on page 98 shows that, broadly speaking, the hypothesis is supported.

On the whole, the relationship between structures, culture and outcome proposed in Chapter Two seems to hold. A true test will be the usefulness of the theory and the empirical evidence it has spawned to a home that is in difficulty. A small experiment at Indigo, for example, would be useful to see if the results of the research can be used to improve what has been, by general consensus, a poor home. The starting point for this exercise will not be, as other managers have tried, group work with the children. Nor will it be, as residential workers have frequently requested, staff training. The starting point will be the societal, formal and belief goals of the home and trying to make these more concordant. That might result in staff training; it might not. It might result in group work, or it might not. It depends on the goals of the home. If that imbalance is corrected, then it is expected that the culture among staff will improve and the culture among residents will either fragment or change for the better. This experiment and others like it should provide a true test of the theory.

Before then, however, it is necessary to complete a last but vital step in the research; to see if outcomes of homes has anything to do with outcomes for individual children.

# 9 Outcomes for homes and outcomes for children

This chapter completes the process of analysis by considering outcomes for the children resident in the nine homes. A placement in a residential home is often just one in a series of interventions experienced by children looked after. In an unpublished Dartington paper, of all admissions into one local authority's children's homes over the period of a year, it was found that, of 78 children, two fifths had been looked after prior to the admission in question, either in other residential placements, foster care or both. In assessing outcomes, it is therefore necessary to look at the 'career routes' of individual children; that is their path through the care process and the interaction of this with home experiences, rather than viewing particular episodes away from home in isolation. By this method, it is usually possible to build up a realistic view of what can be expected or hoped for from any single intervention.

The primary aim of this chapter is to find out whether anything provided by a children's home has given the child anything more than what might reasonably have been expected, given the type of intervention and the characteristics and career route of the child. What is the 'value added'? Did it offer, for example, more than a stay in bed and breakfast accommodation? This way of looking at outcome should lead to residential care being seen as a 'positive choice', contributing something over and above the next best alternative. If there are any benefits, they should become apparent in this part of the exercise. While the long-term effects of residential care are debatable, there is considerable research evidence to show that young people's behaviour is affected by the context while they are there.

The issues involved in evaluating outcomes are manifold and are covered in Parker and colleagues' *Looking After Children* as well as in other Dartington publications, such as the follow-up studies of very difficult and disturbed adolescents. The importance of being clear about the baseline against which outcomes are being measured, the value of looking at the whole child and the benefit of establishing what can be expected within the timescales of the follow-up, be they 6, 12, 24 months or into adulthood, all need to be stressed.

The 65 children resident in the nine homes on the first day of fieldwork were followed up for the year of study. Their progress was measured in three ways; the first, touched on in the previous chapter, concerns the way the residential centres responded to each child; the second uses the *Looking After Children* materials; and the third adopts a technique used in other Dartington studies of comparing what actually happened to children with what might have been expected from research knowledge, given their circumstances when referred to a service. In combination, these methods should give an accurate picture of outcomes for individual children.

## The response to individual children

Initially, the analysis focused on whether the child's needs were clearly defined at the point of entry to the home. The nature of the admissions varied widely, from those that were carefully planned to same day emergency placements. Naturally, there was greater scope for collecting relevant information on a child's needs through a planned admission, although the use made of information collected (however limited) is as important as how it is collected. In some homes, for example Magenta, placements were planned but children's needs ill-defined and knowledge about their circumstances was not fully utilised. Other homes, like Red, took significant numbers of emergency placements, yet managed to collate relevant information and define needs (although at Red these were rarely written down). Of the 65 admissions, only a fifth had their needs clearly defined at the point of entry.

Children's needs should be expressed in a care plan drawn up for the individual *in situ*. The plan should demonstrate how the intervention will meet the child's primary needs - those that led to the child being looked after - and secondary needs - those that arise once a child is being looked after. A victim of abuse, for example, may need some form of counselling. If nobody in the children's home is equipped to provide this, the plan should incorporate details of who will provide it. Less than a third (28%) of the 65 children had such a plan drawn up; this proportion includes the fifth of the children who had their needs clearly defined. The disparity between the two figures demonstrates that some plans were not based on information about residents' primary needs. So, although the majority of the children experienced a statutory review, very few had a plan developed and activated by the homes concerned.

This situation influenced the ability of staff to maintain realistic expectations for the children. What did they believe the intervention could provide and did this match what could be achieved in practice? Such expectations should, of course, reflect available resources and the background characteristics of the children. In homes where sufficient attention was paid to the children's needs and to setting out how these could best be met, staff were realistic about what the intervention could provide. In homes where this was not the case, staff often felt ill-equipped to cope and unable to see what could be achieved within reasonable limits. If expectations were too high, staff were left feeling they had failed and, if they were too low, this affected the messages communicated to the children.

More promising was evidence on clarity of boundaries and consistency of approach. Did staff tell children what was expected of them and did residents receive compatible messages from all members of the staff team? Even before analysing the results, it was clear that the linear relationship between structure, staff cultures and child cultures would bear heavily on the ability of staff to be clear and consistent. In education, for example, societal goals stress the value of school. The ability of staff to support this aim, for example by applauding a child who does well in a school exam will, in turn, affect residents' attitudes to classes including, for instance, truancy. Two thirds (42) of the 65 children were provided with clear and consistent boundaries in most areas.

The scrutiny of outcomes extended to whether residents understood the reasons for their placement. Naturally children's awareness will reflect their intelligence and capability of understanding the nature of the intervention. Those with learning difficulties who were offered respite care at Yellow, for example, required much dedicated work (alongside the children's families) to communicate the role residential care filled in their lives. This enabled the children to feel safe, and most viewed their periods there as fun or holiday time. By comparison, other homes made much less effort, leaving residents to believe they were looked after because they were 'bad' or 'unwanted'. Good understanding was found for just 28% of the children.

Good understanding appeared to lead children to appreciate what the placement could contribute to their lives. In Cyan, Yellow and Red, children were encouraged to recognise the value of particular aspects of the intervention, such as the quality of a certain member of staff or a particular activity. If the children saw the relevance of this to their lives overall (however limited the scope and timescale of the intervention), then a better understanding was fostered. In Yellow many of the children expressed their appreciation through their clear enjoyment of their time there. Some children in other homes articulated the value of specific interventions. Most of those children who kept in touch or chose to visit the home after they had left demonstrated some insight into what the home had offered them. Overall, just 28% of residents saw value in their placement; these were the same children who had developed good understanding of the reasons for their placement.

Children were also asked whether they knew how long the placement would last and where they would go next. In Cyan, for example, where placements were long-term, children were kept aware about plans to move them on when the time was deemed right. For many this meant completing their education at the community before leaving to live again, for example, with previous foster carers. Only 38% of residents had a good sense of the timescale of their placement. Some of the children had an idea of how long the placement was expected to last at the outset but became disillusioned when plans did not come to fruition (and when they saw other children moving on in unplanned ways). The departure of three-fifths of residents lacked a coherence and for 11 the placement broke down.

Finally, the ability of the placement to maintain the children in some form of schooling or employment was examined. As described, this varied greatly from one home where full school attendance was the norm to the next where none of the children went to school and refused to attend their individual tuition. Three quarters (77%) of the children came to the homes with problems related to schooling, such as past truanting or a statement of special educational needs, so extra investment in education was a certain need. Among many strategies tried were good and open communication with residents' schools, school work being sent to the home, staff being encouraged to participate in parent-teacher events or steps being taken to ensure that birth parents could attend. As four-fifths (83%) attended some form of schooling or employment on a regular basis, it appeared that practice in this area may be improving.

The first condition of a good outcome for the children concerned is that homes should respond appropriately to their needs. The factors just reviewed relate to one another; for example, if children have their needs clearly defined this helps in the formulation of a comprehensive child care plan. This plan then helps staff to have realistic expectations and aids children's understanding of the intervention and what it can contribute to their lives. The plan should also help children to move on in a positive way. The crux of all these service factors is the definition of children's needs and the application of these needs in drawing up comprehensive individual child care plans.

## Looking After Children

The principles of the *Looking After Children* approach to outcome measurement are now widely known. The Essential Information and Assessment and Action Records form the fundamental component of the method and provide tools by which a child's overall situation can be measured at different points in time. Seven dimensions of a child's development can be monitored using these records; these are health, education, emotional and behavioural development, family and social relationships, self-care and competence, identity and social presentation. The records are made up of a series of age appropriate forms for six age groups; under one, 1-2, 3-4, 5-9, 10-15 and 16 and over. Ideally the forms are completed collaboratively, with the social worker or residential worker involving the child.

As was explained in Chapter Three, the *Looking After Children* materials were completed on two children in each home. The forms were completed at the beginning and end of the one year study period. There were some difficulties in collecting the information. If the child had moved on after a short period of residence it was difficult to differentiate the effects of the intervention in question from those of subsequent placements and experiences. Neither was it always possible for the residential social worker to complete the forms. Against this, it should be reported that many so called 'key workers' noted how helpful the process had been in providing a format for them to focus relevant discussions with residents.

To illustrate the findings from the *Looking After Children* approach, three children, each from a different home, will be described. The cases concerned are those of Jack, Tracey and Natasha. Jack spent the year in question at Orange, the local authority home that catered for children aged 7 to 12. In theory, Orange also had a specific remit to provide 'therapeutic care' to 'vulnerable, damaged children' and placements were expected to be measurable in years rather than months. Tracey lived in White, which cared for children aged 11 to 16 years. Placements were supposedly for a limited period up to six months in duration, but a significant proportion of the children had already been there for over a year at the start of the study period. Natasha lived in Cyan, the wing of a large therapeutic community. She was selected because she lived in a larger home than the others, and one run by the voluntary sector.

## Jack

Jack's parents divorced when he was a toddler. Their marriage had been difficult and volatile. Jack stayed with his mother and since that time had little contact with his father. His mother had a number of new relationships as he was growing up and gave birth to three more children. Her relationship with Jack was less than tranquil and, at eight years, Jack was fostered by his grandparents. After six months they found his behaviour too difficult to cope with and he was placed in a residential home where he stayed for 18 months. Jack then returned to live with his grandparents but they continued to struggle and at 11 years old he was moved to Orange.

At the beginning of the study period Jack had already been looked after for nearly two years. Orange had provided him with a period of stability and continuity of placement, but there were signs of restlessness. Orange's remit was to meet the needs of younger children, aged 7 to 12 years, and, as Jack grew closer to adolescence, his behaviour stretched the capabilities of staff. Deterioration in many spheres of his life became increasingly marked during the year of study, as the Assessment and Action Records demonstrated.

His *health* needs increased over the year as he became a regular smoker. A very slight child, he did not eat properly and suffered from a number of illnesses, from flu to earache. His problems with *education* came to a peak mid-way through the study year when he was excluded from school. He was offered three hours a week home tuition instead, but he did not even receive this due to his lack of co-operation. His *behaviour* became increasingly difficult and defiant and suspicions grew that he might be abusing drugs and alcohol. He was becoming out of control.

Contact with his grandparents and mother were very erratic and had received little attention. He formed closer emotional ties with a number of the staff at Orange over the year but remained generally unpopular with the children and had no close friends because of his violence. His self-esteem was consistently low and he found it increasingly difficult to behave appropriately in different social contexts. The one area where Jack showed some improvement was in his *self care skills*; he became more confident using public transport and going to the shops alone and more able to carry out basic tasks for himself like making his bed. Overall, though, the picture was depressing.

There was no clear and consistent long-term plan for Jack at Orange. Attention was needed to all areas of his development. During the year a number of potential placements were considered but none came to fruition. He already had a history of rejection and the message that there was nowhere for him to go contributed to his spiral out of control. He had stayed at Orange too long, with detrimental effects, due to a lack of thorough plans to move him on in a constructive way.

Table 9.1: Assessment and action record summary for Jack

| Area of development | Evidence of change | | |
|---|---|---|---|
| | Improvement | Little/no change | Deterioration |
| Health | | | ✓ |
| Education | | | ✓ |
| Emotional/ Behavioural | | | ✓ |
| Family/social relationships | | ✓ (social) | ✓ (family) |
| Self-care/competence | ✓ | | |
| Identity | | ✓ | |
| Social presentation | | | ✓ |
| Long-term plan developed? | No | | |

## Tracey

Tracey was separated from her mother at approximately five years of age, when custody was awarded to her father. Her mother was a prostitute and had not offered Tracey an adequate standard of care. She lived with her father and paternal grandmother for four years, until that relationship too broke down, largely due to her father's heavy drinking. Following a two year period with foster carers she returned to live with her father but the relationship continued to be turbulent requiring 'respite' with Tracey's father's girlfriend.

Tracey's placement at White began as a formal respite arrangement, but soon became permanent as relationships with her father failed to improve. She had been at White for about a month when the study period began. The *Assessment and Action Record* monitored her development between the ages of 13 and 14 years.

Under the sections *education* and *social presentation* some improvement was noted in Tracey's development. She fell within the 'special needs' category at school, and her attainment throughout the year remained 'average' within her group. Her behaviour could be disruptive at times, but she acquired new skills and developed new interests such as extra-curricular courses in arts and crafts and increased involvement in school activities. Tracey became more comfortable in these contexts and able to adjust her appearance and manners to suit them.

However, on the whole, the Assessment and Action Records brought out the lack of significant change in most areas of Tracey's life. Her *self care skills* still needed attention if she was to be competent to care for herself in a way appropriate to her age; she did not cook simple meals or wash up, for example, as this was largely done by the staff. There was little change in her *emotional and behavioural development*, excepting an increase in behavioural problems which could be accounted for by the onset of adolescence. In terms of her health, Tracey continued to smoke and drink alcohol moderately throughout the year. The records showed that there were areas where change could have been beneficial for Tracey, but there had been little input to help bring these changes about.

The main area of deterioration was in her relationships with her family. Contact with her mother had been resumed the previous year after a lapse of four years, but remained sporadic. At the outset, contact with her father was on a weekly basis, but by the end of the year it had become monthly, or less. As discussed, Tracey's placement at White began on a respite basis and, even when it became permanent, the expected outcome was a return to live with her father. During the year of study, deteriorating family relationships led to a shift of focus towards fostering as the most feasible future option.

As with Jack, no clear long-term plan had ever been developed for Tracey. This may explain why the placement lasted longer than intended and why the expected return home did not come to fruition. If a constructive agenda for working with Tracey's father had existed, the picture might have been different. As it was, although Tracey did not fare badly over the year, the picture was marked by a lack of change. This is summarised in the following table.

Table 9.2: Assessment and action record summary for Tracey

| Area of development | Evidence of change | | |
|---|---|---|---|
| | Improvement | Little/no change | Deterioration |
| Health | | ✓ | |
| Education | ✓ | | |
| Emotional/ Behavioural | | ✓ | |
| Family/social relationships | | ✓ (social) | ✓ (family) |
| Self-care/ competence | | ✓ | |
| Identity | | ✓ | |
| Social presentation | ✓ | | |
| Long-term plan developed? | No | | |

## Natasha

Natasha had a disrupted early life. She came from a large birth family, being one of ten siblings. She was fostered by family friends between the ages of 2 and 11 years. The foster father sexually abused her and dressed her up as a middle aged woman, giving her the authority to run the house and to dictate to his wife. At 11 years, she was rescued from this bizarre situation and came to Cyan.

By the time the research began, Natasha was 12 years old. Staff accounts of her behaviour on arrival showed that there had already been much improvement, particularly in her emotional and behavioural development. By the end of the study period, Natasha was entering adolescence, a relevant factor when monitoring her developmental progress.

The Assessment and Action records showed that her health remained good throughout, and that staff were diligent in taking all necessary preventative measures. Natasha was of average intelligence and, although her attainment remained borderline, she attended school regularly throughout the year and started to acquire new skills. She joined a yoga club, which was sociable and helped her to relax, and had started a social skills training course. There was also a marked improvement over the year in her ability to concentrate.

Levels of contact with her birth family were not good at the start of the study period and were little improved by the end. This erratic contact reflected the unstable nature of relationships with her family and the relatively low levels of self-esteem noted may have been related to this area of her life. The situation was slightly more stable with her foster mother and monthly contact was maintained. Natasha's insight into her own situation was good and improved, thanks to the support of staff.

Her attachments with the group at Cyan and those in the therapeutic community improved over the year: stronger bonds grew between herself and the staff (especially her two key workers) and she formed new friendships with the children. At the yoga group she showed an ability to adapt her behaviour appropriately to new contexts. Her sleeping and eating patterns stabilised over the year, which may indicate an increased sense of security.

Questions in the record under the category *Emotional and Behavioural Development* highlighted that, although there was general improvement and increased stability, Natasha still experienced difficulty. A number of aggressive outbursts were noted throughout the year, one of which involved threatening staff with a knife. This occurred just prior to the group's move and was put down to Natasha's anxieties about change. The regularity of such incidents, however, significantly reduced during the year. It would be unrealistic to expect that the path of a young person with Natasha's experience would run smoothly. What was noticeable about her development was her increasing insight into and awareness of her behaviour and the consequences of her actions, as the following diary extract (written towards the end of the year) demonstrates:

It is a sunny Sunday today. I will be round the corner today because last night I punched Jim (staff) for no reason at all but because I wasn't feeling all right I put my anger on to Jim by calling him names and punching him. I did not want to do it but I felt really angry and upset because I punched him and all Jim was trying to do was help me. Sometimes I am such a prat and a fool.

Overall, Natasha developed well and consistently over the year of study, as the following summary table shows. The box added at the bottom of the tables for each of the three children (Jack, Tracey and Natasha) relates to the existence of a long-term plan. However successful the intervention may have been to date, Natasha was still only 13 years when the research stopped. If no plan had been in place then there would be a risk that progress would be reversed. A long term plan to which Natasha had contributed had been designed. The intention was that she should remain at Cyan to complete her education at the community's school and then be fostered back in her local community. Negotiations were already in progress concerning the fostering plans. Natasha would spend time getting to know her potential carers before she moved away from the therapeutic community, although Cyan would continue to offer her informal support after departure.

Table 9.3: Assessment and action record summary for Natasha

|  | Evidence of change | | |
|---|---|---|---|
| Area of development | Improvement | Little/no change | Deterioration |
| Health |  | ✓ |  |
| Education | ✓ |  |  |
| Emotional/ Behavioural | ✓ |  |  |
| Family/social relationships | ✓ (social) | ✓ (family) |  |
| Self-care/ competence | ✓ |  |  |
| Identity |  | ✓ |  |
| Social presentation | ✓ |  |  |
| Long-term plan developed? | Yes | | |

The *Looking After Children* materials were filled in on another 15 children and evidence from these provides similar profiles. At Cyan, for example, George, like Natasha, improved steadily over the year of study. Inevitably there were variations in the details; the records filled in on Jane in Orange showed a scenario that was not as bleak as Jack's. She was still in full-time education, for example, and was managing to cope with the transition to secondary school. Like Jack though, there was no comprehensive plan set out for Jane and deterioration increased as she grew into adolescence. The overall message from applying the *Looking After Children* approach to this study is the importance of the intervention in determining outcomes for individual children, particularly while they are in the homes. Staff should take heart from the better homes: provided staff do not expect miracles, something positive can usually be done, if only to maintain the *status quo*. What the *Looking After Children* approach does not show, however, is whether the progress of individual children was better or worse than expected; did the children who improved do better or worse than their background characteristics suggested they might?

## Outcomes compared to expectation

In a recent Dartington study of very difficult and disturbed adolescents, a method of predicting outcome and comparing children's actual progress with the prognosis was used to some effect. Like *Looking After Children*, it considers the whole child in relation to certain categories of experience, this time living situation, family and social relationships, social and anti-social behaviour, education and employment, physical and psychological health and dependency. At the beginning of the study information was collected in each category to get a comprehensive picture of the child's situation. A prediction was then made, using knowledge gleaned from authoritative research, to set out the likely best and worst possible outcomes for each individual. At the end of the year, the child's 'real' outcome in each category was measured against these parameters. The approach helped to give a sense of what the intervention had contributed to the child's progress.

This method was applied to the same 18 children, two from each home. On this measure, five of these children did generally well or better than expected, three were classed as medium in that they fell somewhere between the best and worst parameters and 10 did generally poorly or worse than expected.

As an illustration of a child who did better than expected, Joe from Red provides a good example. Joe was 16 years old when he was placed at Red. Subject to a care order, he came from another local children's home where they had been having difficulties controlling his delinquent behaviour.

Table 9.4: Joe on entry to Red

| Living situation | Moved to Red (for independence training) from another residential placement<br>Service family - several past moves |
|---|---|
| Family and social relationships | Family breakdown - mother remarried<br>Has older birth siblings<br>Joe does not get on with stepfather<br>Currently no contact with mother or father |
| Emotional and behavioural development | Assault/ABH, theft, TDA and absconding |
| Physical and psychological health | Uses drugs (regular cannabis user) |
| Education or employment | Excluded from school, history of truancy |
| Dependency | Has had two previous foster placements - both broke down<br>In a residential home for three months prior to this placement |

The environment at Red appeared to suit Joe well. His behaviour changed almost overnight; in his previous home he had consistently 'trashed' his surroundings, whereas he respected Red. He enjoyed being treated as an adult in an atmosphere where respect between the staff and young people was fostered. One of the conditions of life at Red was that all the young people must be in a job or training scheme. Staff helped Joe find a job in a local garden centre and he took to it immediately. He maintained his relationship with his girlfriend and this became more stable during his time at Red. He also re-established contact with his mother and his father.

Joe moved on from Red after nine months to live in a flat with his girlfriend. At the last follow up this arrangement was working well. He still used cannabis, but this had reduced and his offending behaviour had stopped. He was enjoying his job and contact with his family was becoming increasingly regular.

The application of the prediction method to Joe, based on the information collected on his situation on entry to Red, set out a generally poor prognosis. Given all of his background characteristics the most likely scenario predicted was that his delinquency and drug habit would escalate and he would find himself in custody. At worst it was possible that he would do something very violent and at best it was hoped that he would re-establish family contacts and that they would help support him. So Joe did better than expected. The protective factors that contributed to a positive outcome were Joe's respect for the environment at Red, the job that he found with their help and his relationship with his girlfriend.

At the other end of the spectrum, Kim did much worse than had been expected. Kim was placed at Magenta when she was 15.

Kim spent 10 months at Magenta, 200 or so miles from her home town. She and her twin Jodie made regular visits home, either in a planned way for contact visits to see their mother, or while running away to go and see 'friends'. There were strong suspicions that during these visits the twins continued their involvement in prostitution.

Kim attended the Magenta school when she was there, but her regular absconding meant that she missed a substantial part of her education programme. Eight months into her placement Magenta moved her to supported lodgings in the local town. This allowed Kim a greater degree of independence and for a short while she seemed to be doing well, attending school and a number of training schemes. Jodie was 'expelled' just prior to this move and, by all accounts, was living in London, having returned to prostitution as a full time career. Kim resisted her sister's invitations to join her there but ran away from Magenta, going home to the North and continuing to prostitute herself.

Table 9.5: Kim on entry to Magenta

| Living situation | Middle class background<br>Lived with mother and twin sister<br>Fostering prior to placement (broke down)<br>Placed at Magenta with twin |
|---|---|
| Family and social relationships | Parents separated (when child aged 12)<br>Both twins became increasingly difficult to control<br>Contact maintained with home<br>No known abuse |
| Emotional and behavioural development | Sexually precocious, self harm, frequent absconding |
| Physical and psychological health | Drinks alcohol and takes drugs |
| Education or employment | Very bright<br>History of truancy |
| Dependency | One previous foster placement (5 months) from which she frequently absconded |

Kim's prognosis based on an assessment of available information on entry to Magenta, highlighted family therapy (with her mother and sister) to be the most likely route to achieving a positive outcome. The best case prognosis was that she would respond well to regular, family therapy and would also be offered psychotherapy. She and her twin would return to live with their mother and they would all receive continued support. Because Kim was bright, it was hoped that education might act as a protective factor. It was also hoped that her academic ability would mean she appreciated the health risks involved in prostitution.

The worst outcome predicted was that she would not receive any form of therapy, the residential placement would become obsessed with control issues (focusing on her running away rather than on her primary needs) and she would return to prostitution. In this way, placement in a secure unit would become likely as she was putting herself at risk of harm. Although at the end of the study it was too early to know if secure accommodation would be requested, Kim's general situation (and experience at Magenta) was less than satisfactory.

The gathering of relevant, comprehensive information on entry, using this to predict the best and worst future scenarios and comparing prognosis with what actually happened revealed a good deal about the ways in which residential interventions contributed to the outcomes for the children.

The five children who did best were all in centres which produced coherent child care plans. All 10 who did worst lacked such a plan. The potential for children to stay longer than was beneficial was a consequence of absence of planning. Drift was a feature in five of the 10 cases where children's outcomes were worse than expected. These children were not necessarily doing badly; most attended school and were quite settled in their placements, but the optimum time for moving them on in a constructive way had passed and they were lingering in a placement that had little to offer. A pro-active approach on behalf of the child was uncommon in these cases, perhaps because staff felt powerless to effect change.

## Relating outcome of children to outcomes for homes

In the previous chapter, ways of looking at the outcome of residential homes were described. These methods were applied to the nine homes in the study and showed three outcome categories - good (Cyan, Yellow and Red), medium (Blue, Green and White) and poor (Orange, Magenta and Indigo). This chapter has provided a separate look at the outcomes for the children who were living in the homes at the beginning of the study using three approaches; whether service factors were met, the *Looking After Children* materials and the prediction exercise.

Did the good homes achieve better outcomes for the children than the bad homes, or was there no significant link? Because of the small numbers of children in each home, figures in the next table must be treated with caution; one child moving categories could alter the figures substantially. Nevertheless, this is the pattern found. Testing the relationships on a micro- level using a large sample of homes and children will undoubtedly lead to qualifications about the generality of the findings. It may even raise doubts about the extent to which good homes produce good outcomes for children. Thus, the results need to be set alongside those of the research by Sinclair and Gibbs and Berridge and Brodie if the relationship between the nature of children's homes and the outcomes for the individual children assessed using independent criteria is to be fully explored.

Table 9.6: Outcomes for children in three areas compared with outcomes for home

| Outcomes for children in three areas | Outcomes for home | | |
|---|---|---|---|
| Service factors met | Good Homes | Medium Homes | Poor Homes |
| (for Ns, see Appendix 2 Table 1) | C 100% | B 27% | O 0% |
| | Y 100%  95% | G 20%  29% | M 17%  6% |
| | R 80% | W 43% | I 0% |
| Looking After Children | Improved 67% | Improved 50% | Improved 17% |
| (n=6 per group) | No change 17% | No change 33% | No change 33% |
| | Deteriorated 17% | Deteriorated 17% | Deteriorated 50% |
| Prediction exercise | Better 67% | Better 17% | Better 0% |
| (n=6 per group) | Similar 17% | Similar 17% | Similar 17% |
| | Worse 17% | Worse 67% | Worse 83% |

## Conclusion

The relationship between a home's structure and culture has already been established; a good structure leads to a concordant staff culture, which in turn leads to a concordant child culture. This chapter and its predecessor, looking at outcomes for homes and the individuals in them, add the final components to the study. They demonstrate that concordance between a home's structure and between the structure and culture (staff and child) results in a good home, and a good home leads to better outcomes for children.

To those familiar with residential work, this may not be too much of a surprise but it is important to have it confirmed using independent evidence. The important contribution is not so much the result but the linear model used to explain it. If this holds, then it has implications for practice. First, it breaks the tautological argument described earlier that has dogged planning in residential care and led to so many false starts. Second, it shows that the focus for reform and improvement should concentrate on the structure, and in particular the relationship between societal, formal and belief goals. Third, it seems that it would be useful for managers to understand this process and to be provided with a practice tool which allows them to apply the model to their own situation. It is this last exercise which forms the basis of the next chapter.

# 10 Practical applications of the results

Data on the nine homes involved in the study have now been analysed. The moment when conclusions can be drawn has not yet arrived but certain findings are apparent. The amount of change in the homes - in staff, residents, aims and objectives, even in the buildings occupied - has been startling. Given claims to offer continuity or stability for children in need, disappointment might be a better adjective. It is also obvious that some homes are better than others at performing the same tasks. Cyan contrasts favourably with Orange and White with Indigo. Such differences cannot be attributed to lack of resource, staff training, support from the local authority or children's backgrounds, the usual explanations of deficiencies in residential care. That children's progress through and beyond these homes has been so varied is also a cause for concern.

Criticising residential care has become *de rigueur* for researchers and, in recent times, journalists adopting the habit. But what would we do if placed in the shoes of managers responsible for residence, those running the homes or residential social workers? What practical messages emerge from the study?

This chapter seeks to provide answers to two questions. First, how does a manager establish a situation where a residential home has concordant structural goals and staff and child cultures that are complementary? (That is to say, in the terms of this study, a good home which achieves benefits for children sheltered). Second, if problems are apparent in the way an existing home is operating, what steps can be taken to achieve a remedy? In addition, it is hoped that the approach set out in this book would uncover potential scandals of the kind that have shaken the residential sector in recent years? Or would a visit to

Beck's home have revealed concordance between structural goals, a supportive staff and a quiescent child culture?

To answer these questions, a different tack from that in the preceding chapters is taken. This structure and culture study is one of several emerging from the Dartington Unit that can be applied to the provision of residential care. Also relevant to the questions just asked is *Matching Needs and Services*, which provides a method to help local authorities decide which looked after children need to be in residence and what that residence should be like. Then there is *Looking After Children* which provides materials to monitor children's progress as they move through residential care and beyond; once aggregated, the data produced by this method should give some insight into the quality of care in any home.

So, to answer the first two questions just asked - regarding the creation of good homes and ways of remedying deficiencies in existing ones - this chapter will set out appropriate structure, culture and outcome measures for groups of children needing residential care. Some comparisons with the nine homes in this study will be drawn.

## How to establish a good home

To begin to answer the question how to establish a good home, it is necessary to ask another-*What are the needs of children to be looked after by this home?* This may be very clear. If the proposed centre is highly specialised, for example catering for 8-11 year old autistic boys or if there has been a thorough assessment of need undertaken on young people thought to be likely candidates for admission, the manager should know or be in a position to discover the necessary information.

This was not the case in the nine homes studied for this book. Nor is it likely to be the case for the majority of children's homes in England and Wales. Cyan undertook a needs assessment but the analysis never rose above the individual. So, well meaning but nonetheless mistaken assumptions were made about the residents; 'oh, they have all been sexually abused' (when most had not) or 'oh, none will be able to go home' (when most will). In Red, the task was reasonably specialised - adolescent boys who had fallen out with parents and then with substitute carers. But the understanding of the educational, employment, social and health needs of these young people was limited.

*Matching Needs and Services,* in the version prepared for the Department of Health's Support Force for Children's Residential Care, is designed to establish the needs of looked after children. It can be applied across a local authority or within one area. It uses information on all children being looked after in one year to plan services for those requiring care or accommodation the next. Application in several local authorities has consistently highlighted the need for residential care, ensuring the service has a focused and positive function and does not become a repository for the detritus of needy children that fail to find safe havens elsewhere. It also tries to show how residence in combination with other Part III services can address children's needs. Properly applied, the method should indicate which children are best placed in which home, how long they are likely to stay and to where they will be expected to go next.

This is not the place for a description of the method. Suffice to say that it can be applied over a matter of weeks. What is outlined here are two of the need groups that consistently appear when local authorities have applied the *Matching Needs* method (there are ten described in the publication). The two selected serve to illustrate what the approach, in combination with the ideas offered in this book and the application of the *Looking After Children* materials, can achieve.

> The first group comprises adolescents whose frequent rows with parents had necessitated a short period away from home. The need was to give parents and the young person some respite from each other while maintaining important continuities in the young person's life, particularly school, work experience, reasonable health and orthodox social networks. In Derbyshire, for example, which is not untypical of English local authorities and serves a child population of about 200,000 with about 500 of these beginning to be looked after by social services departments each year, there would be between 45 and 70 young people with such needs.

> The second group consists of young people aged over ten who had experienced unsatisfactory parenting, exacerbated by mental health problems and criminality, over many years, including frequent separations from home. The need was for consistency of care in a place where the child would settle. High levels of contact eventually leading to a reunion with relatives was a

necessity. In a typical local authority in England, there will be 25 children with such needs.

Having established dominant need groups, such as the two described here, the next task is to define a combination of services which will best meet those needs. These decisions are best made collectively involving managers, professionals and consumers. There are also benefits from consulting the latest research evidence and considering the principles which underpin the 1989 legislation set out in *An Introduction to the Children Act*. In one typical local authority piloting *Matching Needs and Services*, the following results emerged:

> The first group should be given a choice of residential care or foster services. On the basis that two will choose residence for every one selecting a foster home, the demand for places would be 50 per annum. Entry to accommodation would be offered on the strict understanding that a return to relatives should occur within four weeks. Given that demand for places would not be even, it can be calculated that eight beds would be required. External mediation services would be sought to ease relationship difficulties between parents and child. Two homes of four beds would be ideal in the typical authority, thus obviating control problems caused by large groups which can deflect from the primary aim of the homes. Homes would be close to the parental home and school or good transport would be arranged to maintain links with the young person's neighbourhood. Homes would be firm about attendance at school, the participation in mediation and maintenance of family links but reasonably liberal in other respects.

> The second group required long-term placements with expert psychotherapy to address children's deeper needs. Consumer testing had indicated that one in every two children in this group will not want to live in another family context, thus necessitating a placement like Cyan. In a typical local authority, about 10 young people each year would therefore require such a placement. The demand is probably insufficient to justify the social services department directly providing the service. Emphasis should be placed on the ordinary aspects of a young person's life; of social and cultural events; of education; of good health care. But much effort would also need to be invested in giving the young person and his or her family insight into their difficulties and to the young person coming to understand that

he or she is not responsible for problems that have occurred at home. Stability will be vital to reasonable outcomes, meaning that the residential centre will have to adopt a non-rejection policy or, in plainer language, put up with considerable amounts of disruption. Stays of two to three years would be the norm for such young people. However, they may choose to move on to relatives or foster placements as they progress into adolescence and the residential home should accommodate such change as long as it does not cause problems in other areas, particularly education.

If this broad definition of the service to meet the different needs of children being looked after is accepted, the next step is to set out the structural goals of the placement. To an extent, this will have been part of the previous analysis since, presumably, the intervention has been designed with the *Children Act* principles in mind. But more detailed work is required to establish the societal, formal and belief goals of the home. Again, certain aids can help. The most important of these will be *The Care of Children* which sets out the 42 principles and the practice regulations and guidance associated with the *Children Act, 1989*. They are listed in Appendix 6. Volume Four of the guidance is also essential reading. Consultation with the research evidence, particularly *Residential Care: A Review of the Research* and the studies which have emerged from the Department of Health's recent programme of investigation into residence will be helpful.

In practical terms, a reasonable way forward is to set out a grid such as those in Tables 10.1 and 10.2. Down the vertical axis are the principles of the *Children Act, 1989* as set out in *The Care of Children* (just 4 of the 42 principles have been selected for the purpose of this illustration but in practice all the principles should be incorporated). Across the top axis are three sets of questions which will establish roles, responsibilities and review procedures in respect of each *Children Act* principle. So the grid requires the managers to reflect on:

- what, who, where and how questions about the application of each principle

- what support will be needed (e.g. through supervision and training) to ensure these tasks will be done, and

- what review procedures exist to see if the principle is applied.

Table 10.1 represents the grid completed for the first need group of adolescents whose frequent rows with parents had necessitated a short period away from the parental home.

**Table 10.1: Needs and services for adolescents experiencing difficult relations with home**

| Children Act principle | What, who, where & how? | What support is needed? | What review procedures? |
|---|---|---|---|
| When out of home care is necessary, active steps should be taken to ensure a speedy return | 1 Children should feel safe from discontinuities that have characterised childhood. | 1 Staff to be trained in research on separation and return and in the handling of access visits. | 1 Child and parents' behaviour to be monitored prior to, during and immediately after access. |
| | 2 Initial access to take place in children's home so that parents can feel welcome. | 2 Field social worker to prepare parents for visits and take care of travel arrangements. | 2 Field and residential workers to review planning for each access visit two days after the last visit. |
| | 3 All participants to know that reunion and at least high levels of contact is highly probable in the long-term. | 3 Parents and children to be prepared for anxieties concerning access as well as separation and return. | 3 Access and eventual return plans to be an agenda item at each review. |
| Time should be reckoned in days and months rather than years | 1 Young people's daily progress to be monitored for anxiety associated with long term discontinuity. | 1 Training for staff in research on continuity and discontinuity. | 1 Daily log. |
| | 2 Young people's progress to be monitored against natural developmental expectations using Looking After Children materials. | 2 Key workers to be employed in expectation that they will stay for as long as the child. | 2 Weekly summary prepared by the key worker and copied to the field social worker and communicated to the family. |
| | | 3 Training for all staff in use of Looking After Children materials. | 3 *Looking After Children* Essential Information, Care Plan and Assessment and Action Records. |
| Corporate parenting is not good enough on its own | 1 Identification of two family members outside of the parental home with whom the child can keep in touch. | 1 Key worker to visit family and field social worker for two or three days at beginning of placement. | 1 Key worker to debrief with supervisor. Plans to be checked with family and child. |
| | 2 Maintenance of childhood friends in home neighbourhood. | 2 Appropriate supervision and support from management for the above. | 2 Managers to visit with staff the parents' home and neighbourhood. |
| | 3 Development of orthodox links in immediate vicinity of children's home. | 3 Children's homes to establish good links with the local community. | 3 Open day annually to include community suggestions for home's development. |

## Table 10.1 *cont'd*

| Children Act principle | What, who, where & how? | What support is needed? | What review procedures? |
|---|---|---|---|
| Young people's wishes should be taken seriously | 1 Use of group work so that young people can express themselves to each other.<br><br>2 Independent visitor to visit monthly. | 1 Training for all staff in listening to young people and responding to children's needs.<br><br>2 Training for all staff on the role of an independent visitor and or/Guardian ad litem. | 1 Child to be given role in the selection of an independent visitor.<br><br>2 Material emerging from groups to be reviewed for consistency and development of emerging information.<br><br>3 Place to be found for independent visitor in the review procedure. |

## Table 10.2: Needs and services for young people experiencing unsatisfactory parenting

| Children Act principle | What, who, where & how? | What support is needed? | What review procedures? |
|---|---|---|---|
| When out of home care is necessary, active steps should be taken to ensure a speedy return | 1 A family group conference to be convened to agree terms of accommodation or trained mediator employed to enjoin agreement of family members.<br><br>2 Going Home checklists to highlight factors necessary for swift reunion. | 1 Trained FGC co-ordinator or mediator to offer support.<br><br>2 All staff to be trained in separation and return and in use of Going Home checklists.<br><br>3 Field social worker to monitor changes in family home and liaise with key residential workers.<br><br>4 Transport as necessary to and from home. | 1 Parents and young people to contact each other (at least) at week 1 and every other day thereafter.<br><br>2 Parents to visit young person and review targets set at 7 day intervals.<br><br>3 Field and residential social workers to meet for 30 minutes each week and talk by phone once a week.<br><br>4 Driver to report to key residential worker. |
| Time should be reckoned in days and months rather than years | 1 Care plan to set out expectations for young people for each of the 28 days of residence.<br><br>2 Long-term prognoses set out following work of family group conferences or mediator. | 1. Manager to monitor plans to ensure they are achievable.<br><br>2 Training for all staff on care plans and supervision for new recruits. | 1. Manager to review young person's progress against plan once a week.<br><br>2 Key worker, young person and family members to do likewise. |

**Table 10.2** *cont'd*

| Children Act principle | What, who, where & how? | What support is needed? | What review procedures? |
|---|---|---|---|
| Corporate parenting is not good enough on its own | 1 Care plan should include provision for maintaining, retrieving, beginning school or work.<br><br>2 Residential worker to get to know youth network in young person's neighbourhood. | 1 A teacher or employer to act as a link worker and to participate in the setting of targets.<br><br>2 Transport to and from school and employment.<br><br>3 Advice from education, police and community services. | 1. Residential social worker to visit teacher after school once a week.<br><br>2 Driver to report to key residential worker and know teacher.<br><br>3 Young person's orthodox social network to be reviewed before and after residential sojourn with a view to it widening. |
| Young people's wishes should be taken seriously | 1 Young person should determine as many clauses in contract as do professionals.<br><br>2 Young person to be asked to select key workers after three days residence.<br><br>3 One significant adult outside residence to be identified as confidant. | 1 Training for all staff in listening to young people and responding to ordinary adolescent anxieties.<br><br>2 Family Group Conference co-ordinator or mediator to have skills in listening to young people. | 1 Contingency plans to be built should young person disclose abuse or admit serious offence. |

Table 10.2 repeats the exercise for a home catering for young people aged over 10 who had experienced unsatisfactory parenting over a number of years. It is not necessary to go through the detail of these exhibits. It will be seen that they are very specific to the needs of the child. It will be apparent that the content of the tables differs because different needs are being addressed. The links between the boxes, both horizontally and vertically, should also be clear.

Through this mechanism, a children's home can be built on the twin foundations of the needs of the child and the principles of the *Children Act*, 1989. By reading down the columns, it should be possible to estimate how many staff will be needed, what their skills and qualifications should be, what training and supervision arrangements need to be put in place and what review and recording requirements are necessary. Naturally, not all that is desired will be possible and priorities will have to be set to ensure that the principal needs of the child are always met and that secondary needs are addressed whenever possible.

The exercise should also include contingency plans. What will happen, for example, in the home dealing with adolescents rowing with parents if the young person breaks the contract, either by going home early or refusing to go back at the end? What happens when members of staff are off work through sickness or stress? In the long-stay home, which has a non-rejection policy, what happens if a young person causes extensive damage to the fabric of the home? Each of these potential difficulties will be familiar to experienced managers and it should be possible to have in place plans to obviate possible crises.

The formal goals of the children's home should emerge through this process. By default, these objectives should accord with the societal goals for children in need manifest in the principles of the *Children Act, 1989*. Some of these formal goals should be written down in a form accessible to staff, residents, parents, outside professionals and other visitors to the home. Others can remain implicit but managers need to know how goals are to be communicated and met.

The manager must believe that these goals will meet the needs of children, satisfy the principles of the Act and are achievable within available resources. If the manager has organised the process just described, any doubts that arise can be properly addressed and resolved to his or her satisfaction. To skip through the method proposed here would be to run the risk of leaving open sores which will later be picked by staff and residents and require remedial surgery.

This process of establishing formal goals should also make apparent the cultural response from staff and residents. In the home for adolescents frequently rowing with their parents, consensus among staff about frequent contact, regular attendance at school, doing homework, the role of the mediator - what might be thought of as the core elements of this particular residential experience - would be essential but disagreement about peripheral matters, say which television programmes young people should watch, could be tolerated. As residents' stays in the homes are expected to be short, the cultural response of young people will likely be fragmented and it would seem advisable to put in place strategies that ensure that the group's anger with parents is not transferred to staff. In the longer stay home, consensus among staff and children across all areas of the home is manifestly more important.

There is no single method of setting out a desired cultural response of staff and residents, nor of evaluating whether intended group dynamics actually occur. The following diagram uses the tasks described in Appendix Three to formulate questions to be asked of a manager designing a children's home. Only five questions are asked for the purpose of this illustration, but it would be possible to have another 20. To give an idea of how it might work, answers have been given in respect of the two hypothetical homes described above to meet the needs of adolescents out of sorts with their relatives and younger children who require longer-stays away from home to establish some continuity in their lives.

Table 10.3: How a manager can build up a picture of culture in the children's home that is concordant with the structural goals

| Tasks in the home as questions* | Short-term adolescents | Long-term younger children |
|---|---|---|
| How should staff behave when a resident is about to leave the home? | The departure will be a major source of anxiety for young person and family alike. The departure must not appear like the end of the intervention. Rather, the young person is taking another step towards rapprochement with home. All staff to be supportive and to use departure as an opportunity to learn for the next leaver. | The departure will make a significant moment in the life of the home (only two children will leave each year). The move should be treated as a rite of passage but all staff should be expected to pay particular attention to the anxiety the event will create for the child and his or her family and for the children's home itself. |
| How should residents behave if they know another resident has been distressed by an access visit? | There would be no expectations of residents' behaviour in this respect in this home other than they did not increase tensions. | It would be expected that such tensions would be the subject of discussion in the child's group. |
| What should staff do if one resident assaults another? | Assaulting staff would be a breach of contract in this home. There should be some collective discussion about how to react with the final decision made by manager in conjunction with key worker, field worker, young person and family members. Staff would be expected to support this decision. | An assault is a serious attack on the safety of residents. It must be treated seriously, necessitating group meetings of staff and residents. On the other hand, the no rejection policy requires that a meeting of minds occurs. Monitoring effects on behaviour of all residents is essential. |
| How would residents be expected to behave if someone refuses to go to school? | All residents will know that school is a high priority for the home and a non-negotiable part of the contract. On the other hand, it is not expected that residents should pass judgement on each others' behaviour | Residents would not be expected to comment on behaviour at time of occurrence but it would clearly be the focus of a child group meeting taking place after school that day. |
| What should staff do if a resident is complaining of illness at breakfast? | One staff member, preferably the key worker, would take responsibility. Other staff members would go about their usual tasks. | One staff member, preferably the key worker, would take responsibility. Other staff members would go about their usual tasks. |

*These questions are adaptations of those listed in Appendix Three

The final steps in this method are to set outcome targets and strategies to review the performance of the home and individuals within it. The process described in this chapter should provide the manager with sufficient information for an annual plan for the home, stating how many children will be sheltered during the year as well as what will be expected to happen to them during their stay and afterwards. In the first home this might be monitored by way of a quick telephone call to the young person's field social worker or parents a year after departure. In the second home more elaborate procedures, such as an application of the *Looking After Children* materials, would be advisable. Similar targets and reviews could be put in place for staff employed by the home. The residential centre as a whole could also be evaluated using some of the criteria for good homes described in Chapter Eight. Much of this could take the form of a business plan which external advisers inspect each year to measure what has been achieved and what might be improved.

Of course, such evaluation should be regarded as integral to the design of the home and costed as such. This will pose a dilemma of how many resources should be devoted to this part of the task of looking after children. In a large successful business, some 5 to 10% of expenditure will go on research and development. In the National Health Service this proportion is 1%. In the personal social services, the percentage drops again, to maybe less than 0.1%.

Two homes sheltering eight adolescents who have rowed with their parents, assuming stays of four weeks and an occupancy rate of 90%, would shelter some about 70-100 young people each year. Following up ex-residents would therefore take one person about three weeks' work, perhaps four if a short report were produced. At face value, this seems quite a burden on the limited resources of a children's home. But it represents less than half of one per cent of staff time (assuming it takes 20 people to run the homes) and should be of considerable value to the next 100 young people being looked after. Indeed, a home failing to find out what happens to its ex-residents might be thought of as unprofessional.

So, there are several stages in the process of establishing a good home. There are, in addition, many methods of going about the job. Those proposed above are well known to Dartington, but there will be others that complete the task just as well. The steps can be summarised as follows:

Table 10.4: Stages and methods in the process of establishing a good home

| Stages in process | Possible Methods |
|---|---|
| 1) Establish a residential service that, in combination with other Part III services, meets the needs of children being looked after in a locality. | Matching Needs and Services |
| 2) Set out the formal and belief goals of the home which meet the needs identified in stage one and concord with societal goals for children in need. | The principles of the Act taken with the roles, responsibility and the review grid set out in tables 10.1 and 10.2 above. |
| 3) Establish a staff and child culture which complements the structure of the home (as specified in 2). | The culture pro-forma as set out in Table 10.3. |
| 4) Set in place procedures to create targets for the home, residents and staff as well as methods to review whether these targets are met. | Looking After Children for long-stay cases. Simpler methods for short-stay homes. |

## Finding remedies to existing problems

Few managers have the luxury of designing a new home. Most inherit centres that 'have a history'. It is increasingly common for this bequest to have problems that require sorting out. The methods suggested in the preceding section should, with time, begin to clarify the locus of difficulty. Is it in the structure of the home, the formal and belief goals? Or are there cultural problems that might be remedied through changes in staffing or communication? If nothing else, the preceding chapters have established that there is little point in tampering with the group dynamics of the resident group if there is discord between society's aims and the manager's objective for residential care.

When the programme of matching needs and services and designing a congruent structure and healthy cultures is undertaken, it is helpful initially to consider the future of the children already resident. A second exercise can be undertaken independently of the first to sort out the problems of a home in trouble, for example, Indigo as described at different stages of this study.

The starting point is the current needs of the residents. These are highly likely to be a combination of needs identified at the point the child was first looked after and secondary needs that have arisen in the context of their care since separation. Where a home is in crisis, these secondary needs may be quite severe, including running away, a refusal to see relatives, delinquency or violence, drug abuse or self harm and, almost certainly, a refusal to participate in school. These secondary needs were apparent in all the troubled homes included in this study and many of those surveyed by others as part of the Department of Health research programme.

These needs should be recorded in a swift exercise involving residential and field staff. The same dimension of living situations, family and social relationships, social and anti-social behaviour, physical and psychological health, education and employment used on the *Matching Needs and Services* exercise will help. Where information is recorded on *Looking After Children* forms, it can be extracted using the following formula.

Table 10.5: Relationship between *Looking After Children* and *Matching Needs and Services* categories

| Looking After Children categories | | Matching Needs and Services categories |
|---|---|---|
| | | Living situation |
| Family and social relationships | equivalent to | Family and social relationships |
| Self care skills | | |
| Identity | | |
| Social presentation | all equivalent to | Social and anti-social behaviour |
| Emotional and behavioural development | | |
| Health | equivalent to | Physical and psychological health |
| Education | equivalent to | Education and employment |

The second stage is to select a period of time appropriate for the needs of the child during which some reasonable progress can be expected; that is to say when all the secondary needs and some of the primary needs will have been addressed. The period may be short - say three to six months - in relatively straightforward cases, but long - two or even five years - in a more complex situation.

Using the identified primary and secondary needs in each of the five areas (from living situation to education and employment) of the child's life, the aim of the second stage is to set out what can be reasonably achieved within the chosen time period. Research evidence may be helpful in determining this. For example, it would be misleading to assume that a child who has been refused contact with relatives will quickly return home because the evidence demonstrates this to be highly unlikely. Neither can we expect a persistently delinquent adolescent to stop offending because almost certainly he (occasionally she) will not.

The third step is to consider what services would achieve these desired outcomes. It may be that the residential home in which the child is resident plays a part in the next step; it may not. On the other hand, the most likely scenario is that residence alone will be insufficient. The interaction between needs and services to meet these needs should have become apparent during the first two stages of the work. An example, commonly found in homes in crisis, is of a reduced misbehaviour when education or employment needs are met, so occupying the young person and integrating him or her into a wider social network.

All three stages in the process should take no longer than a day for each resident with a second day allocated to consult the child, his or her family and the professionals required to make the plan work. A statutory review will be required to complete the process.

The benefits of this exercise for a home in crisis are also considerable. First, it can be used rapidly to settle the children down. It may result in some residents being quickly moved on but it should avert the calamity of the home temporarily closing with harmful consequences for children and staff.

Second, it will identify and precisely quantify the service, say psychological help or an educational placement, and the training, for example in restraint techniques, that staff will require in order to achieve the outcomes set for current residents.

Third, it will move the children on from the problems that beset the home at the point of crisis in a constructive way. They should, therefore, come to recognise the limits of acceptable behaviour within the establishment and not be shunted on to another home triumphant that they 'closed the place down'.

Finally, it should regenerate staff morale as they see the crisis through and resolve some of the problems that produced it in the first place.

Cyan has been useful in illustrating the strengths and weaknesses of the approach emerging from this study. It has been found to be one of the better homes. Its aims and objectives also seem appropriate for the second of the need groups identified above, namely children who had experienced unsatisfactory parenting over an extended period. But when the predictive techniques just described were applied to Cyan residents, several gaps in the provision of care emerged.

First, while the majority - if not all - the residents were eventually likely to return to live with relatives, the goals of Cyan mostly focused on the life of the child within its walls. So while many transitions to parents were handled successfully, planning was left until the moment that the child had exhausted Cyan's resources. Consequently, residents suffered unnecessary anxiety and parents sensed they were unwelcome within the therapeutic community. The principle expressed in *The Care of Children* regarding contact was seldom mirrored in the formal goals.

Second, the multiple needs of children resident were evident yet Cyan was tardy in using the expertise of others outside its perimeter to meet them. Indeed, unless other professionals used the opaque language of psychotherapy they were often dismissed as irrelevant. So it sometimes happened that a psychologist would be drawn into a care plan when it was a housing officer that was needed or the psychotherapist's sand-tray was preferred to the much needed support of the class teacher in the local mainstream school. So much for the *Children Act* principle that the various departments of a local authority should co-operate to provide an integrated service and range of resources, even when such co-operation is not specifically required by law.

Third, it became clear that Cyan was poor at taking into account the wishes of the children. The home certainly listened to the children but it did not always hear their wishes, especially if these contradicted the social work plan. Thus, residents saying they wanted to move - or, for that matter, to stay - only had their wishes addressed when words coincided with deeds, for example, a refusal to go to school, an attack on another resident or running away.

These structural deficiencies in Cyan had consequences for the culture. If the very strong likelihood of reunion were to be addressed, then parents would have to be made welcome by staff and children. If connections with other support agencies were to be meaningful, the principles of psychotherapeutic working would have to be challenged, or at least extended. If children's wishes were to have some legitimacy, the dynamics of group meetings around which life in Cyan revolved would have to be changed.

It is important to bear in mind that Cyan was a good home and achieved good outcomes on behalf of the children it looked after. The observations just made imply a potential for further improvement; a possibility that might be measured if the outcome techniques described above were put in place. The application of the approach to Cyan also highlights some deficiencies in the ideas that have informed this book. The methods are rather cold and clinical. They miss much that is warm and intuitive. What Cyan missed in terms of its understanding of the *Children Act,* 1989, it made up for with an enveloping blanket of support woven over half a century of caring for troubled children.

## Conclusions

This chapter has tried to apply the results of the research in the nine homes to those charged with the difficult task of establishing, managing and inspecting residential centres. A proposal has been made to further refine these tools and test them on a small group of typical children's homes. The principal aim of this modest exercise would be to summarise in one booklet and in a form useful to managers the techniques described. A spin-off would be a prospective testing of the findings. It should be possible to use such a practice tool to turn around a home in trouble. It should also, in theory, be possible to use the approach to measure and to improve outcomes in a small children's home. In combination with *Matching Needs and Services, Looking After Children* and other development tools emerging from the Department of Health's research programme, it should be possible for any local authority to plan an effective residential care service.

# 11 Conclusions

The focus of this book has been the structure (defined as the orderly arrangement of social relationships within the home, governed by its societal, formal and belief goals) and culture (taken to mean the shared understandings of staff and residents, particularly as manifest in group responses to specified events) in children's homes. Interest in the relationship between these two aspects of residential homes follows a long tradition of institutional studies which reached its zenith in the 1960s. From this work the term, 'formal and informal worlds of staff and residents' - the original title of this study - was borrowed. But residence has changed, as has our knowledge about who goes into children's homes, where they go afterwards and the context in which the service is offered. New concepts, methods and connections were required to understand the contemporary residential scene.

Nevertheless, the inheritance from these earlier studies is a number of clear messages for policy and practice. Regimes have a considerable effect on children's behaviour while they are resident and welfare oriented approaches have consistently been found to produce better results for children's health, education and personal social development. Staff and child cultures have long been known to influence outcomes even if the precise nature and direction of the association has been difficult to determine. Until now, the principal conclusion from this evidence was that managers should ensure that cultures did not cohere in a negative and destructive way. While some of these results from two decades ago were encouraging for professionals, other hopes such as for enduring behaviour change in offenders were dashed. Nevertheless, the features of effective homes, providing good quality care, were reasonably well established and have been summarised in several publications.

But the usefulness of these findings for managers and staff charged with making residential care work has been limited. Even homes seemingly well planned from the start have failed to succeed. A list of correlations between structural variables and outcomes is difficult for managers to interpret, especially when the message is more a case of what should not happen than a clear indication of what needs to be done. Nor are the global descriptions used in previous Dartington summaries, such as the notion of a 'good home' or putting together a 'positive culture' or a 'favourable ethos', of much value in the melée of daily residential life. It has not helped that many previous research messages were fashioned prior to *The Children Act*, 1989 which sets out a framework for the care of children and views the role of residential care in the context of a continuum of services for all children in need. As in life itself, everything in residential care can seem to be related to everything else. Emphasising single features stifles much rational discussion. How many times has the tautology 'a good home is one which has a good manager' or 'a good home is one which is a happy home' been heard by policy makers, researchers and practitioners involved in the Department of Health's programme of studies? A contribution from research was needed if we were to learn what a manager actually has to do to achieve a good home. This study attempts to do this in several ways.

First, it sets out a linear model of cause and effect which argues that, in children's homes at least, structure determines staff culture which determines child culture, which in turn determines outcome for homes and residents. While there is obviously some feedback in the process, the research was able to discount the possibility of the opposite situation where cultures determine structures. The sequence described is the model that best fits the data.

The second contribution has been the focus on the homes themselves and the ways in which they change. The inclusion of nine homes prevents the dangers of generalising from single cases. The monitoring of change has freed the research from the constraints of our predecessors who looked at residence as a static entity, hoping to capture its impact on those who lived and worked there. Most important of all has been the assessment of outcomes based on measures that can be independently tested. This and the linear relationship between structure, culture and outcome, breaks the study free from the circular arguments and tautologies just described.

Outcomes for homes and for the children in them clearly show that some homes do better than others and that observed differences cannot be explained in terms of single factors, such as the background characteristics of children and staff.

The approach has required a range of research data. Critics might suggest that some of the measures are somewhat 'soft' and that some of the assessments are made by those who developed the theory in the first place, so questioning the validity of the findings. Such a danger is almost inevitable when dealing with the intangible aspects of residential life but some safeguards have been incorporated. Independent researchers, in addition to the two employed on the project, visited each home. The measures employed, such as rates for running away, staff absence, the construction of care plans and the *Looking After Children* Assessment and Action Records, are relatively objective. Results have only been presented if they are supported by all of the evidence collected for this study and by much other research. Nevertheless, it is only by having the results re-tested by managers applying the emerging research tools that we can be fully satisfied with the reliability of the relationships described.

Nine homes were studied, a selection which provides a representative view of residential homes for children looked after. They were visited a year apart and several times in between so that a complete picture of staff and child cultures could be compiled. Eighteen of the 65 children resident at the time of the first visit were studied intensively over time. Changes in fortune were a feature both of the homes and the children. It was depressing to find that so much effort of reorganisation and refurbishment had little ostensibly to do with improving services or implementing more fully the *Children Act,* 1989. The homes are still very isolated from mainstream child care and the wider principles that underpin the legislation. It was surprising to find that abuse disclosures, falling rolls and staff redundancies were not major pressures for change.

Change, like all other components in this model, has good and bad effects, encouraging improvements in the better homes but exacerbating difficulties elsewhere. Change in itself is not sufficient to lift standards in the poorer homes although, self-evidently, it is necessary to improve practice. Without knowing its effects or what it is supposed to achieve, much innovation is wasted. Is it best to empty a bad home and start again, or is more training or a new leader the answer? The difficulty is knowing where in the chain of effects to intervene.

From the perspective of this study, the starting point must be the different goals-societal, formal and belief-of the children's home It is the relationship between these goals, the evidence suggests, that determines staff and child cultures. Thus, if goals are out of balance or the relationship is contradictory, no amount of work on staff and child cultures will improve the situation. By providing managers with a methodology to assess and understand this relationship better it should be possible to raise standards.

Societal goals have been defined as those shared principles and ideas about the ways children are raised, including children in need. *Residential Care,* Volume Four of the *Children Act* Guidance, lays out what should be done and how. Formal goals are the aims and objectives of each home and represent an interpretation of the societal goals to meet local conditions and the particular needs of the children being cared for. *The Care of Children: Principles and Practice in Regulations and Guidance* has been shown to be an effective tool in clarifying the formal goals of a home. Belief goals encompass what the manager fundamentally believes about what the home can do for its residents, including the capability of staff.

The homes presented a varied picture with three (four by the time of the second visit) showing high concordance between the three sets of goals, three displaying some ambiguity and two where there was obvious discord. The remaining home presented a mixed situation. The relationship between the three types of goal determined how the homes responded to change, that is whether they were forward and progressing or generally deteriorating. Chapter Ten presents a practical model which not only helps promote concordance but also ensures that practice is based on the twin foundations of the needs of the child and the principles of the *Children Act,* 1989. If the findings of this exercise are complemented by attempts to link homes to other services for children in need and to a method of assessing outcomes, a management model that leads to good care for children should be established. It is hoped that by reviewing social, formal and belief goals in this way, abusive cultures that have been long known but ignored are exposed and dealt with.

The study goes on to explore the relationship between structure and culture, culture being defined as a group response to a set of problems and tasks common in residential care. The study began with the hypothesis that structures influence staff cultures which, in turn, influence child cultures. Generally, this relationship has been proven, although some of the links were not quite as direct as just described. For example, the strength of cultures was found to vary. In five of the nine homes, staff cultures were strong; in three they were medium and in one they were weak. The values they supported and the areas of concern also differed. Child cultures, in contrast, were less evident. In only two homes were they strong and positive, in four they existed but were weak and in three more hardly apparent. This situation probably reflects the variety of children's past experiences and their isolation from peers.

Four patterns of relationship between structure and culture were found. The first occurred in three homes. Here, high levels of structural concordance caused a healthy staff culture which supported the aims and objectives of the home and maintained either a strong or a fragmented child culture.

A second pattern was found in three homes where discord in structure produced some problems in culture. Staff and child responses were mixed both in terms of strength and orientation, thus limiting the achievements of the home, but not too disastrously.

In two homes, highly discordant structures caused staff cultures to be strong and counter productive. In one of them, the child culture was very negative indeed, encouraging delinquency and acting out that had serious consequences for the young people. In the other home, the child culture was relatively weak, though still very negative.

One home did not fit the model, displaying a reasonable degree of concordance in its structure but with weak staff and child cultures.

Thus, the concordance between societal, formal and belief goals predict with considerable accuracy the strength of the staff cultures and the support those cultures bring to the aims and objectives of the home. It has been slightly less successful at predicting the nature of child cultures, perhaps reflecting the varied background characteristics of the residents and the small size of the living group.

In children's homes, strong cultures are not necessarily bad. Indeed, staff can benefit from the insights and practical help offered by positive peer support and managers can use this strength, along with training and supervision, to further the work of the home. Child cultures are more difficult to manage but a strong culture can complement the work of staff provided children implicitly understand the goals of the establishment, comprehend the way their particular home implements these and perceive senior staff as people able to achieve something on their behalf. In such situations, there is no need to fragment the child culture. Thus, another hardy annual of residential care theory is modified in the light of carefully gathered evidence.

So much for the findings on structure and culture. How does this help with the tautology that a good home is a home that is good? Outcomes had to be measured, both for the homes themselves and for the children. Twelve indicators of the homes' performance emerged, exploring how staff, children and other visitors see the home; how staff and children are observed to behave in the home; and, how good was the practice relative to the standards specified by the *Children Act*, 1989. The test applied concurred with that used by other projects in the Department of Health programme. When these indicators were applied, it was clear that homes which did best on nearly all the criteria employed were those with concordant societal, formal and belief goals, strong positive staff cultures and either strong positive child cultures or ones that were fragmented without undermining the work of the establishment.

The outcomes for children were also measured in several ways. These included the extent to which their needs were identified and addressed, whether they understood the reasons for their placement and its duration, whether education and employment were maintained and the quality of care plans. For a quarter of the children, two children in each home, more detailed assessments of children's progress were made. The *Looking After Children* materials were used to chart changes in children's situations and assess outcomes. In addition, a method used in previous Dartington studies whereby actual outcomes are compared with predictions of best and worst scenarios, based on authoritative research knowledge at the point of admission to the home, was employed. Again, on nearly all these measures, while some children did better than others, they all did best in the better homes; thus completing the final link in the explanatory model.

When children are looked after, there is a danger that deficiencies in the care placements will exacerbate the deprivation and harm that necessitated separation from their families. A child doing badly in residential care needs a good quality intervention, not transfer to another poor quality home. System neglect whereby the needs of children remain unmet is less pernicious than physical or sexual abuse but is no less dangerous. Evidence from this study and the early application of the *Looking After Children* materials confirm this. So, how can the situation be improved?

1. There is little benefit in looking at homes in isolation. There may be organisational changes which may improve matters, such as better record keeping or more effective communication, but this is unlikely to be sufficient to lift a home out of the doldrums or to guarantee high standards.

2. There has to be an initial understanding of the needs of the children being looked after in the home. This was not common among the homes studied, resulting in opinionated generalisations about children's situations and limited action in areas such as health and education.

3. There has to be an understanding of how residence is one of many means of meeting the child's needs. An appropriate package of services, shown by research to be the most effective known, has to be compiled.

4. With this knowledge in mind, the structural goals of the home need to be set out. Societal and formal goals based on the principles that underpin legislation, as set out in *The Care of Children*, pave the way. For each one, managers need to reflect on how the principles apply to a particular home and what resources are needed to put them into practice. This can only be done relative to the needs of the children and remedial services identified. Needs and *Children Act* principles are thus combined in the process of defining and setting the formal goals.

5. Appropriate staff responses should become clear as goals are formulated. This, the study argues, will lead to functional child cultures. This approach is helpful because it evaluates cultures relative to the needs of the children and not as something universally good or bad.

6. Goals should be evaluated by assessing how far the homes achieve set targets indicated by research as likely to be achieved for each needs group.

Residential homes are powerful environments. Their effects on children's behaviour and thus on their welfare are considerable. It is only by taking the broad view suggested in this study that needs, services and outcomes can be effectively related. The next task is to use these ideas as a basis for practical tools that allow managers to explore these relationships. When these are in place, the accountability that should accompany good management can be enforced and professionals, families and children, and the public at large, can be more confident about the welfare of young people looked after in residential care.

The opening pages of this study were written in a hotel lobby, the host to a conference on the strengths and weaknesses of residential care. The gathering has finished and the delegates have dispersed, leaving behind a few researchers who have unfinished work, now joined by a handful of holiday makers determined to enjoy their winter weekend away. Laid bare since the majority of its residents have departed, one begins to see this 'home' for what it is. A carefully evolved structure which makes possible a culture suitable for the blinkered academic, honeymoon couple and bargain break weekender alike. Only those unwise enough to question 'why are these staff being so nice to me?' should encounter any difficulty. Distanced from its enticements, we begin to ask who is this hotel for? What does it seek on behalf of its residents? What do staff have to do to make these goals achievable and how should guests get on with each other? How would the manager know if the hotel is operating well or badly or whether customers are satisfied? These questions apply equally to children's homes. Indeed, a cold detached look on behalf of that small proportion of children in need who require residence - asking about need, structure, culture and outcomes - will undoubtedly help, along with the abstract deliberations of the academics at the conference just ended, to ensure that the needs of vulnerable children in residential care are being properly met.

# Appendix 1: References

The preceding report is not peppered with references to the work of others. Residential care has been well researched and there was a danger that every sentence would require acknowledgement of one source or another. So a plainer style of presentation was selected.

An overview of the preceding literature is provided in *Residential Care for Children: A Review of the Research* published by HMSO in 1993. This draws out common findings from 117 studies, reviews and reports and shows how these have contributed to the understanding of process, services and outcomes in residential child care. There is little in the HMSO review about structure and culture and much reading was undertaken to get a better grasp of these concepts. It is difficult in retrospect to pinpoint exactly where the ideas used in the study came from but the following description gives an indication.

As the body of a research unit's work grows, it is possible to identify consistent intellectual reference points. Three are worth mentioning here. We take from Karl Popper's *The Poverty of Historicism* what might be thought of as a sceptical positivism in the sense that methods used in the natural sciences are applicable but there remain considerable doubts about questions of inference and proof. We take from Michael Rutter's studies the proposition that rigorous science can be applied to a discussion primarily concerned with the individual, even when that discipline is more interested in belief than cold evidence. Finally, we take from Rom Harré, for example in his *An Explanation of Human Behaviour*, the prospect that qualitative methods can be subjected to the same analytic rigour as quantitative methods. In this sense, there is a place for the so-called hermeneutic tradition mentioned in Chapter Three, although the extent to which the analysis of meaning could be built into the concepts used in this study has been limited.

This was the background to the reading about structure and culture. Invariably, any exploration of new concepts begins with Merton's consistently useful *Social Theory and Social Structure*. There was also much to draw on the structural side of the equation from *A Manual to the Sociology of the School*.

Culture was more difficult. The definitions of 'culture' and 'structure', too rely heavily on Gouldner's 1957 article in the *Administrative Science Quarterly* but, as important in the formative stage, were the articles by Becker, Geer and Hughes listed below. Once the ideas took shape, Little's *Young Men in Prison* bore upon the fashioning of a working method as did Becker's article on problems of inference and proof. The writings of Argyle were especially influential on the final model. Once a draft report had been written, we had the opportunity to learn from recent writings, such as Dorothy Whitaker and colleagues' study on *The Prevailing Culture and Staff Dynamics in Children's Homes*.

Other references cited in the text.

Argyle, M. (1967), *The Psychology of Interpersonal Behaviour*, Harmondsworth, Pelican.

Becker, H. (1967), 'History, culture and subjective experience', *Journal of Health and Social Behaviour*, VIII, pp.163-176.

Becker, H.S. and Geer, B. (1960), 'Latent culture: a note on the theory of latent social roles', *Administrative Science Quarterly*, V, pp 304-13.

Becker, H.S. (1970), 'Problems of inference and proof in participant observation', in Filstead, W.J., (ed.), *Qualitative Methodology*, Chicago, Rand McNally.

Brannen, J. (ed.) (1992), *Mixing Methods: Qualitative and Quantitative Research*, Aldershot, Avebury.

Dartington Social Research Unit (1994), *The Part Played by Career, Individual Circumstance and Treatment Interventions in the Outcomes of Leavers from Youth Treatment Centres*, Dartington.

Dartington Social Research Unit (1995), *Children Admitted to Seven Residential Homes in County C*, Dartington.

Dartington Social Research Unit (1995), *Matching Needs and Services: The Audit and Planning of Provision for Children Looked After by Local Authorities*, Support Force for Children's Residential Care.

Department of Health (1989), *The Care of Children: Principles and Practice in Regulations and Guidance*, London, HMSO.

Department of Health (1989), *An Introduction to The Children Act*, London, HMSO.

Department of Health (1995), *Child Protection: Messages from Research*, London, HMSO.

Department of Health (1994, 1995), *A Strategic Planning Framework Part 1 - Analysing Need and Part II-Implementing Change; Staff Supervision in Children's Homes; Good Care Matters: Ways of Enhancing Good Practice in Residential Child Care*, Support Force for Children's Residential Care.

Department of Health (1996), *Children's Homes at 31st March 1995*, London, HMSO.

Department of Health (1996), *Children Looked after by Local Authorities: Year ending 31st March 1995*, London, HMSO.

Gooch, D. (1996), 'Home and away: the residential care, education and control of children in historical and political context', *Child and Family Social Work*, I, pp.19-32.

Gouldner, A. (1957), 'Cosmopolitans and locals: Towards an analysis of latent social roles', *Administrative Science Quarterly*, II, pp 281-306.

Hammersley, M. and Atkinson, P. (1983), *Ethnography: Principles in Practice*, London, Routledge and Kegan Paul.

Harris, M. (1990), *Unholy Orders: Tragedy at Mount Cashel*, Harmondsworth, Viking.

Hatfield, B., Harrington, R. and Mohamad, D. (1996), 'Staff looking after children in local authority residential units: the interface with child mental health professionals', *Journal of Adolescence*, XIX, pp127-139.

Hughes, E., Becker, H., and Geer, B. (1958), 'Student culture in medical school', *Harvard Educational Review*, XXVIII, pp 70-80.

Kahan, B. (1995), *Growing Up in Groups*, London, HMSO.

Lambert, R. and Millham, S. (1968), *The Hothouse Society*, London, Weidenfeld and Nicolson.

Lambert, R., Millham, S., and Bullock, R. (1970), *A Manual to the Sociology of the School*, London, Weidenfeld and Nicolson.

Little, M. and Kelly, S. (1995), *A Life Without Problems: The Achievements of a Therapeutic Community*, Aldershot, Arena.

McCann, J., James, A., Wilson, S. and Dunn, G (1996), 'Prevalence of psychiatric disorders in young people in the care system', *British Medical Journal*, CCCXIII, pp1529-30.

Mead, G. (1934), *Mind, Self and Society*, Chicago, University Press.

Merton, R.K. (1957), *Social Theory and Social Structure*, Glencoe, Free Press.

Parker, R., Ward, H., Jackson, S., Aldgate, J. and Wedge, P. (eds.) (1991), *Looking After Children Assessing Outcomes in Child Care*, London, HMSO.

Rowe, J. and Lambert, L. (1973), *Children who Wait*, London, ABAFA.

Rowe, J., Hundleby, M. and Garnett, L. (1989), *Child Care Now*, London, BAAF.

Rutter, M., Maughan, S., Mortimore, P. and Ouston, J. (1979), *Fifteen Thousand Hours: Secondary Schools and their Effects on Children*, London, Open Books.

Sinclair, I. and Gibbs, I. (1996), *Quality of Care in Children's Homes*, University of York.

Social Services Inspectorate, (1992), *Corporate Parents: Child Care Services in 11 Local Authorities*, London, Department of Health.

Social Services Inspectorate (1993), *The Effects on Residential Child Care Staff of Investigations of Abuse*, London, Department of Health.

Thomas, W., see discussion of theorem in Merton, R. (1957), *Social Theory and Social Structure*, New York, Free Press.

Ward, H. (ed.) (1995), *Looking After Children: Research into Practice*, London, HMSO.

Whitaker, D., Archer, L. and Hicks, L. (1996), *The Prevailing Cultures and Staff Dynamics in Children's Homes*, University of York.

Whipp, R., Rosenfeld, R. and Pettigrew, A. (1989), 'Culture and competitiveness: evidence from two mature UK industries', *Journal of Management Studies*, XXVI, pp 561-585.

Whyte, W. (1943), *Street Corner Society*, Chicago, University Press.

# Appendix 2: The background characteristics of children and staff

Table 1: Characteristics of the children in each home

| | Total | B | Y | G | R | M | O | C | I | W |
|---|---|---|---|---|---|---|---|---|---|---|
| No. at start | 65 | 11 | 5 | 10 | 5 | 6 | 6 | 9 | 6 | 7 |
| Gender | 40 male 25 female | 7 male 4 female | 3 male 2 female | 6 male 4 female | 5 male | 6 female | 5 male 1 female | 5 male 4 female | 5 male 1 female | 4 male 3 female |
| Ethnicity | 50 white 6 Afro/Car. 4 Asian 5 mixed | 1 white 6 Afro/Car. 3 Asian 1 mixed | 5 white | 8 white 2 mixed | 5 white | 5 white 1 mixed | 6 white | 9 white | 4 white 1 Asian 1 mixed | 7 white |
| Legal status | 2 remand 25 care ord. 38 vol. | 1 remand 7 care ord. 3 vol. | 5 vol. | 2 care ord. 8 vol. | 1 remand 1 care ord. 3 vol. | 3 care ord. 3 vol. | 4 care ord. 2 vol. | 7 care ord. 2 vol. | 1 care ord. 5 vol. | 7 vol. |
| Emergency/ planned | 19 emerg. 46 planned | 5 emerg. 6 planned | 5 planned | 6 emerg. 4 planned | 1 emerg. 4 planned | 6 planned | 6 planned | 9 planned | 2 emerg. 4 planned | 5 emerg. 2 planned |
| History of delinquency | 9 | 1 | - | 1 | 3 | 1 | - | - | 3 | - |
| Known to have been abused | 32 | 5 | - | 7 | 1' | 1 | 6 | 9 | 2 | 1 |
| Main reason for admission | 38 bpc 5 offending 4 death of parent 12 abuse 5 respite 1 education | 3 bpc 3 death of parent 1 offending 4 abuse | 5 respite | 6 bpc 4 abuse | 2 bpc 3 offending | 5 bpc 1 offending | 3 bpc 3 abuse | 6 bpc 1 abuse 1 death of parent 1 ed. | 6 bpc | 7 bpc |
| Res./care before | 15 | 5 | - | - | 3 | 3 | - | 2 | 2 | - |
| Foster care before | 17 | 2 | 2 | 2 | 1 | - | 4 | 3 | - | 3 |
| Res. and fost. care before | 21 | 3 | - | 5 | - | 3 | 2 | 4 | 4 | - |
| Not looked after before | 12 | 1 | 3 | 3 | 1 | - | - | - | - | 4 |

## Table 2: Characteristics of the staff (all homes)

| | Total staff at beginning of study | Total staff at end of study | Staff stayed throughout | Part time staff at beginning of study | Full time staff at beginning of study |
|---|---|---|---|---|---|
| Orange | 17 | 14 | 9 | 0 | 17 |
| Red | 12 | 12 | 9 | 1 | 11 |
| White | 8 | 7 | 6 | 0 | 8 |
| Blue | 16 | 18 | 15 | 1 | 15 |
| Indigo | 16 | 14 | 8 | 0 | 16 |
| Green | 22 | 22 | 12 | 7 | 15 |
| Yellow | 14 | 18 | 12 | 7 | 7 |
| Cyan | 9 | 7 | 6 | 0 | 9 |
| Magenta | 9 | 4 | 2 | 0 | 9 |
| | 123 | 116 | 79 | 16 | 107 |

## Table 3: Characteristics of staff in each home

| Homes | No. at start | Gender | Ethnicity | Age 20s | Age 30s | Age 40s | Age 50+ |
|---|---|---|---|---|---|---|---|
| Orange | 17 | Male - 6 Female - 11 | All white | 4 | 8 | 5 | 0 |
| Red | 12 | Male - 6 Female - 6 | All white | 0 | 6 | 4 | 2 |
| White | 8 | Male - 2 Female - 6 | All white | 2 | 2 | 1 | 3 |
| Blue | 16 | Male - 4 Female - 12 | White - 4 Black - 12 | 2 | 5 | 4 | 5 |
| Indigo | 16 | Male - 8 Female - 8 | All white | 6 | 5 | 3 | 2 |
| Green | 22 | Male - 14 Female - 8 | White - 19 Black - 3 | 6 | 6 | 10 | 0 |
| Yellow | 14 | Male - 2 Female - 12 | All white | 3 | 4 | 7 | 0 |
| Cyan | 9 | Male - 4 Female - 5 | White - 8 Black - 1 | 5 | 3 | 1 | 0 |
| Magenta | 9 | Male - 3 Female - 6 | All white | 0 | 4 | 5 | 0 |
| Total | 123 | Male - 49 Female -74 | White - 107 Black - 16 | 28 | 43 | 40 | 12 |

## Table 4: Characteristics of staff in each home

| | Staff at start of study | Staff with social work qualifications | Manager with social work qualifications | Other relevant qualifications | Previous residential experience |
|---|---|---|---|---|---|
| Orange | 17 | 2 | 1 | 3 | 10 |
| Red | 12 | 0 | 0 (1 by end) | 2 | 5 |
| White | 8 | 0 | 0 | 1 | 2 |
| Blue | 16 | 2 | 0 (1 by end) | 2 | 15 |
| Indigo | 16 | 1 | 1 | 7 | 10 |
| Green | 22 | 0 | 1 | 1 | 14 |
| Yellow | 14 | 0 | 1 | 9 | 13 |
| Cyan | 9 | 1 | 0 | 6 | 2 |
| Magenta | 9 | 0 | 0 (1 by end) | 4 | 0 |
| Total | 123 | 6 | 4 at beginning 7 by end | 35 | 71 |

# Appendix 3: Indicators of staff and children's cultural responses and results from the nine homes

Staff and child culture tasks

Living situation

1. A new child arrives at the home.
2. A child leaves the home.
3. Two or more residents have a trip out of the home.
4. A child has a birthday.
5. It is Christmas Day, Boxing Day, New Year's Day or Easter Sunday.

Family and social relationships

6. A parent visits his or her child at the home.
7. A child is reluctant to go home for a visit planned for today.
8. A child in the home has a boy/girlfriend and brings him/her into the home.
9 A child talks about his or her sexuality.
10. Two children are seen being very affectionate to one another.

Social and antisocial behaviour

11. A child behaves in a way that necessitates restraint.
12. A child assaults another child.
13. A child steals from another child.
14. A child brings drugs into the home.
15. A child is dirty and needs a bath.

Education and employment

16. A child refuses to go to school.
17. It is a child's first day in a new school or job.
18. A child comes back from school with homework.
19. A child says that he or she is being bullied at school.

20. A child mentions an event at school or work (e.g. a sports day or play) to which parents are invited.

Physical and psychological health

21. A child complains of stomach ache and does not want to go to school.

22. A child is physically sick.

23. It is announced that a child with a recognised disability is to join the home in four weeks time.

24. A girl says she wants to go on to the 'pill' or a boy asks for contraceptive advice.

25. A child wets the bed.

The tables on the next two pages show the strength and nature of the staff and child cultures in the nine homes. A tick ✓ indicates a cultural response was found amongst the group. A cross ✗ is used when no group response was found. If a cultural response was supportive to the goals of the home then it was regarded as positive. If the response worked against the goals then it was negative. In some instances, either where responses were ambivalent, or where there was no group response and the adults or children were divided in supporting or undermining the goals, then the term 'neither' is used to describe the nature of the culture.

# Table 1: Staff cultures - strength and direction

| | B | Y | G | R | M | O | C | I | W |
|---|---|---|---|---|---|---|---|---|---|
| **Living situation** | | | | | | | | | |
| 1 | ✓+ | ✓+ | ✓+ | ✓+ | x– | ✓= | ✓+ | ✓+ | ✓+ |
| 2 | x= | ✓+ | x= | ✓+ | x– | x= | ✓+ | x– | ✓+ |
| 3 | x= | ✓+ | ✓+ | ✓+ | ✓+ | ✓= | ✓+ | ✓– | ✓+ |
| 4 | ✓= | ✓+ | ✓= | ✓+ | ✓+ | ✓+ | ✓+ | ✓+ | ✓+ |
| 5 | x= | ✓+ | ✓+ | ✓+ | ✓+ | ✓+ | ✓+ | ✓– | ✓+ |
| **Family and social relationships** | | | | | | | | | |
| 6 | ✓+ | ✓+ | ✓= | ✓+ | x– | ✓+ | ✓= | ✓+ | ✓+ |
| 7 | x= | ✓+ | x– | x= | x= | ✓– | x– | x– | ✓+ |
| 8 | ✓+ | ✓+ | x– | ✓+ | x– | x– | x– | x– | ✓+ |
| 9 | x= | ✓+ | x= | ✓+ | x– | x– | x– | ✓– | ✓+ |
| 10 | ✓= | ✓+ | x= | ✓+ | x– | x– | x– | ✓– | ✓+ |
| **Social and antisocial behaviour** | | | | | | | | | |
| 11 | ✓+ | ✓+ | ✓+ | ✓+ | ✓+ | x– | ✓+ | ✓+ | ✓+ |
| 12 | ✓– | ✓+ | ✓+ | ✓+ | x– | x– | ✓+ | ✓= | ✓+ |
| 13 | ✓+ | ✓+ | ✓+ | ✓+ | x– | x– | ✓+ | ✓= | ✓+ |
| 14 | x– | x= | x– | ✓+ | x– | ✓+ | ✓+ | ✓= | ✓+ |
| 15 | x= | ✓+ | ✓+ | x= | x– | x– | ✓+ | ✓+ | ✓+ |
| **Education and employment** | | | | | | | | | |
| 16 | ✓+ | ✓+ | ✓+ | ✓+ | ✓+ | ✓– | ✓+ | ✓– | ✓+ |
| 17 | ✓+ | ✓+ | x– | ✓+ | ✓+ | ✓– | ✓+ | x= | ✓+ |
| 18 | x= | ✓+ | x= | ✓+ | ✓+ | ✓– | ✓+ | x– | ✓= |
| 19 | x= | ✓+ | x= | ✓+ | ✓+ | ✓– | ✓+ | x– | x– |
| 20 | x= | ✓+ | x= | ✓+ | x= | ✓– | ✓+ | x– | x– |
| **Physical/psychological health** | | | | | | | | | |
| 21 | x= | ✓+ | x– | ✓+ | x– | x– | x– | x– | x= |
| 22 | x= | ✓+ | x= | ✓+ | x– | x– | ✓+ | ✓+ | x= |
| 23 | ✓+ | ✓+ | ✓+ | ✓+ | x– | x– | ✓+ | ✓= | ✓+ |
| 24 | ✓+ | ✓+ | ✓+ | x– | x– | ✓– | ✓+ | ✓= | ✓+ |
| 25 | ✓+ | ✓+ | ✓= | x– | x– | x– | ✓+ | x– | ✓+ |
| **Total** | 13 | 24 | 13 | 21 | 8 | 13 | 20 | 16 | 21 |
| | medium | strong | medium | strong | weak | medium | strong | strong | strong |
| | neither | positive | neither | positive | negative | negative | positive | negative | positive |

## Table 2: Child cultures - strength and direction

| | B | Y | G | R | M | O | C | I | W |
|---|---|---|---|---|---|---|---|---|---|
| **Living situation** | | | | | | | | | |
| 1 | x= | x= | x= | ✓+ | ✓= | x− | ✓+ | ✓− | ✓+ |
| 2 | x= | x= | x= | x= | x= | x= | ✓+ | x= | x= |
| 3 | ✓+ | ✓+ | x= | ✓+ | ✓+ | x= | ✓+ | ✓− | ✓+ |
| 4 | x= | x= | x= | ✓+ | x= | ✓+ | ✓+ | x− | ✓+ |
| 5 | x= | ✓+ | x= | ✓+ | x= | ✓+ | ✓+ | ✓− | ✓+ |
| **Family and social relationships** | | | | | | | | | |
| 6 | x= | ✓+ | x= | ✓= | x= | x− | ✓+ | x= | ✓− |
| 7 | x= | x= | x= | ✓= | ✓− | x− | x= | x= | ✓= |
| 8 | x= | x= | x= | ✓+ | x= | x= | x= | ✓− | x= |
| 9 | x= | x= | ✓− | ✓+ | x= | x= | x= | x= | ✓− |
| 10 | x= | x= | ✓− | ✓+ | | x= | x= | x= | x− |
| **Social and antisocial behaviour** | | | | | | | | | |
| 11 | ✓+ | ✓+ | ✓+ | ✓+ | x= | ✓− | ✓+ | ✓− | ✓+ |
| 12 | x− | ✓+ | ✓= | ✓+ | x− | x− | ✓+ | ✓− | ✓= |
| 13 | ✓+ | x= | ✓+ | ✓= | x= | ✓+ | ✓+ | ✓− | ✓+ |
| 14 | ✓− | x= | x= | ✓+ | ✓− | x= | ✓+ | ✓− | ✓− |
| 15 | x− | x= | x= | ✓− | ✓+ | x= | ✓+ | x= | ✓= |
| **Education and employment** | | | | | | | | | |
| 16 | x− | x= | ✓+ | ✓− | ✓+ | x− | ✓+ | ✓− | ✓+ |
| 17 | x= | x= | x= | ✓+ | x= | x= | ✓+ | x= | x= |
| 18 | x= | x= | ✓+ | x= | ✓+ | x− | ✓+ | x= | x= |
| 19 | x= | x= | ✓= | x= | x= | x= | ✓+ | x= | x= |
| 20 | x= | x= | ✓= | x= | x= | x− | ✓+ | ✓− | x= |
| **Physical/psychological health** | | | | | | | | | |
| 21 | x= | x= | ✓= | ✓= | x= | x= | x= | x= | x= |
| 22 | x− | x= | ✓= | x− | x= | x− | ✓+ | ✓− | x= |
| 23 | ✓+ | x= | ✓= | x− | x= | x= | ✓+ | ✓+ | ✓+ |
| 24 | x= | x= | ✓= | x− | x= | x− | ✓+ | x= | ✓− |
| 25 | x= | x= | ✓+ | x= | x= | x= | ✓+ | x= | ✓− |
| **Total** | 5 | 5 | 14 | 17 | 7 | 4 | 20 | 12 | 16 |
| | weak | weak | medium | strong | weak | weak | strong | medium | strong |
| | neither | positive | neither | positive | negative | negative | positive | negative | neither |

# Appendix 4: Cultural responses to the same incidents in the nine homes

Cultures varied across the nine homes both in strength and in the nature of the responses. The following tables show how the homes varied in their staff and child cultures in two tasks, 'a child has a birthday' in the area of living situation, and 'a child physically assaults another child' in the area of social and anti social behaviour.

Table 1: A child has a birthday

| Home | Staff response | Child response |
|---|---|---|
| Cyan | ✓ Staff all give individual present and card. Party with games and cake carefully planned for individual child. | ✓ All children give carefully made and wrapped presents and cards. Make it a special and exciting day for all the home. |
| Yellow | ✓ Practice is consistent. Staff all mark the day as special and mark the occasion with cards, tea and an outing. | ✗ Staff encourage children to think of the birthday child, but few recognise this event nor would see need to respond at all. |
| Red | ✓ All staff sign a card and join in trip to pub, or chosen birthday treat, even those off duty. | ✓ Weak response but they all join in the pub visit and wish the child well. Unlikely to buy card etc. or organise anything themselves but they do expect staff to arrange something. |
| Blue | ✓ Weak response. They behave differently for old and new children. For old residents, cake and cards, for new it is no big deal. Only staff on duty celebrate the day. | ✗ Ambivalent and apathetic. Memories of past birthdays are poor so they ignore the event. In some of the different cultures, birthdays are viewed as less important. |
| Green | ✓ Weak response. Low key celebration with a staff card and possibly a cake at tea. Only duty staff involved. | ✗ Staff try to get children to buy a card but the children see no point in marking the day. It has no relevance for the group. |
| White | ✓ All celebrate together with a big tea party. Off duty staff often join in celebrations. | ✓ Card and presents from the group. Is seen as important for the birthday child and fun for all. |

151

## Table 1 *cont'd.*

| | | |
|---|---|---|
| Magenta | ✓ Staff do make a real effort to make the day special. Buy a big present for the child and celebrate with trip out or treat of some kind chosen by the birthday girl. | ✗ No consistent response. Depends very much on whose birthday it is. Some long stay residents will receive cards and presents from the others. |
| Indigo | ✓ All staff do try to mark the occasion. Keyworkers give cards. Attempt to arrange trip out or treat which they believe is unlikely to go ahead as children sabotage it. Only duty staff attend anyway. | ✗ Children apparently do not care. They spoil and sabotage any celebration attempts. Do not give cards or gifts. |
| Orange | ✓ Child chooses a treat and staff give cards. Duty staff only go on treat. Whilst individual staff do take considerable trouble to make the day special, majority view event dispassionately and professionally. | ✓ Weak response. Some might give a present or card. All look forward to the treat or outing and see birthdays in terms of the outing. |

## Table 2: A child assaults another child

| Home | Staff response | Child response |
|---|---|---|
| Cyan | ✓ Stop the assault and discuss event at length in meetings involving staff, children and outsiders. | ✓ Children stop the fight too. All agree this is wrong. Afterwards they discuss together with staff all the reasons leading up to the incident, avoidance strategies and feelings etc. |
| Yellow | ✓ Confident, assured and consistent. Staff know they will all stop the fight and discuss how to stop event ever being repeated. | ✓ If children are physically able they too stop the assault. They are shocked and disturbed by violence. They get staff to help quickly. |
| Red | ✓ Treat the children as adults until they overstep the mark. Fighting is not on. They intervene quickly and effectively and consistently then discuss event with participants until dispute is resolved. | ✓ Children definitely disapprove of violence inside the home. Outside, is different. They support staff to stop the fighting and discuss it afterwards. |
| Blue | ✓ However, response is discordant with goals. Staff ignore it if possible and then restrain if situation continues. Try to discuss afterwards but often this is not deemed appropriate and the incident is closed. | ✗ Depends on who is fighting and why. Other children want to see justice prevail. They do not join in the fight but sometimes take sides verbally and see fighting as justifiable in some instances. |
| Green | ✓ Consistent and confident staff response. Stop the fight. No more discussion, the incident is closed. | ✓ Children are scared by violence so the group try to stop fighting. Some will run away and hide. There is no discussion afterwards, the incident is swept under the carpet. |

# Table 2 *cont'd.*

| White | ✓ Fighting is rare and staff strongly disapprove. They stop the fight and then review whether the violent child is appropriately placed with them. Child is likely to be moved on. | ✓ Response depends on the personalities involved. Some unpopular children might 'deserve' a beating. Afterwards child group meetings are used to resolve disputes. |
|---|---|---|
| Magenta | ✗Violence shocks some staff into inaction and others into action. They are neither confident nor consistent in how they respond. All disapprove, but violence is seen as a dreadful crisis. Staff cannot understand why girls should behave so appallingly. | ✗ Some join in, others ignore or observe or encourage. There is no consistent response. |
| Indigo | ✓ If they have seen it they will all intervene to restrain and separate the participants. They then retire to the office as soon as possible and do not discuss the incident with the children in case the violence resumes. | ✓ This is a signal for all to join in and challenge the staff. Fighting can escalate to the majority of the group. Individuals may watch on the periphery but not join in to inflame or stop the fight. |
| Orange | ✗ Varied responses are possible depending on who is fighting, who is on duty and when the incident occurs. Some over react and call case conferences, other under react and ignore the fight. | ✗ Some ignore or retreat whilst a minority will get involved. There is no discussion afterwards of why or how the dispute might be resolved other than by violence. |

✓ - indicates that a group response was evident. The nature of the response is described in the text.

✗ - indicates no group response.

# Appendix 5: A replication study in the USA by Gordon Bazemore and Kim Gorsuch

*Structure and Culture in Residential Care* concludes with an explanatory model that links the components of children's homes and explores their relationship with outcomes, both for the homes and for the children who live in them. The details have been laid out in Chapter Nine.

If this model is to be more than an elaborate description of institutional processes, several conditions have to be met. Three are especially important. First, different people presented with the same data have to reach the same conclusions. This was achieved in the research arrangements discussed in Chapter Three by the way the teams that visited the homes were organised and the method of analysing the evidence. Second, the model should be applied to new situations to see if the outcomes it predicts are achieved. If this is the case, the model linking structure and culture has applicability beyond the nine homes discussed in this book.

A third way of assessing the model's value is to apply it to homes where the key variables are different from those found in England and Wales. An example would be children's homes in another country; as there would be no *Children Act* 1989, the societal goals might not only be less specific but also different. As societal goals are the starting point of the model, the question thus raised is, does another set of societal goals lead to relationships between structure and culture different from the ones found in the research?

An opportunity for such an exploration arose in 1995. Professor Gordon Bazemore of Florida Atlantic University and a specialist in children's residential care worked at the Dartington Unit on a three month sabbatical. He became familiar with the structure/culture study and decided on his return to North America to apply the methodology to Broward, his local county. For this exercise, he was joined by a colleague who had no prior knowledge of the Dartington project.

## The Florida homes: a description

Two very different homes were chosen for examination. These homes were by no means representative of the array of residential programmes for children and youth even in Broward County. However, the choice of a residential facility for young, generally non-delinquent girls and a secure custody drug treatment facility whose beds were filled primarily with relatively serious delinquent boys was an attempt to maximise diversity in the case studies. While these homes shared important structural similarities that differentiated them from their UK counterparts, the description below establishes clear differences between the homes as well.

### Brown House

Brown House is a private not-for-profit secure drug treatment facility. While the programme in the past served young males referred from different sources, including parents and the young people themselves, during the course of this study all residents were delinquent boys committed by the Department of Juvenile Justice. The programme administrator reported that he 'had little screening authority or right of refusal over referrals but did not object to the target group, believing that the facility should serve relatively serious offenders.'

Seventeen young men ranging in age from 14 to 18 were in residence at the beginning of the 12 month observational period in winter, 1995. This number fluctuated between thirteen at the lowest point in summer, 1996 to nineteen at the end of the period. At the beginning of the study, three of the young men were black, four were Hispanic and the rest were Caucasian. This overall ratio did not vary significantly during the year.

Over the course of the research, there were on average 25 full and part-time staff, not including domestic and maintenance workers. Management and professional staff included the administrator, an operations manager, clinical director, case manager, senior therapists and a family therapist. Several of the therapists worked split or part-time shifts and the family therapist held a part-time consultant position. The other professional was the school teacher. 'Milieu counsellors', who supervised the young men throughout the day and evening, were generally not professionally qualified in terms of having degrees in social work, counselling or related subjects.

On the first visit, researchers were impressed with the fact that this was not a 'home' as such but a facility for housing delinquents who would otherwise choose not to be there. Although staff were 'laid back' and casual, the dorms where the residents lived were at least semi-secure and residents could not leave the grounds unescorted except for approved home visits with parental supervision. The facility had a small yard and recreational areas but otherwise there was little common space. The young residents lived in one of three dorm rooms that housed up to six boys and appeared well kept. They took meals in a small but institutional-type kitchen.

Management and professional staff seemed very informal and relaxed on the first and subsequent visits and they appeared to maintain this attitude with the young residents who wandered in and out of the business and intake offices during the day. This group seemed very much in synch philosophically throughout the case reviews that were observed and they appeared to be friends outside the workplace. If there was a staff culture it would appear to coalesce around these shared values and, to some extent, the new age/1960s lifestyles of the group.

The milieu counsellors shared some of this lifestyle but displayed less commitment to a particular treatment model. Because they worked alternate shifts with two counsellors on duty at any one time, there was little opportunity for interaction with other staff that allowed for the development of a strong staff culture.

While the counsellors seemed committed to the work - several put in overtime and weekend hours voluntarily and the pay was low - there was some resistance, expressed by several counsellors and confirmed by the administrator, to the preferred interactive style with clients which was being encouraged by the administrator. Part of the resistance was over what some counsellors viewed as inadequate pay and the belief that their traditional methods of enforcing discipline (through more coercive use of the points system discussed below) would no longer be available to them.

## The Keys

The Keys was located in a small duplex house in West Broward county. This building housed the two primary staff, a married couple whose job title was 'teaching parent' (TP) and their two children in one half of the building and up to five residents in the other. The home was intended to serve teenage girls between the ages of 12 and 16. But during the time of research the five girls in residence ranged from a 17 year old to a girl of ten transferred from another programme operated by the same agency. Three of the girls in residence were white, one was Hispanic and one African-American.

The girls in The Keys had been referred from various sources, some from within the network of programmes operated by the parent agency. The programme seemed to prefer teenage girls referred for mental health (rather than conduct disorder) problems and who exhibited a medium range of emotional disturbance. The teaching parents asserted that they generally had at least had one girl in residence at any one time who had more severe difficulties than the model was equipped to handle.

The programme was viewed by its director as 'the first step into the system, before kids get into serious difficulties'. The purpose of the programme was to 'teach kids to make choices'. They provided a lot of structure in the beginning (including intensive therapy if needed) but the goal was to get the young people to develop internal structure. The director and staff insisted that The Keys was no longer based on a behavioural model but rather on one that combined reinforcement and feedback with a strong therapeutic overlay.

Children who had some type of family involvement but who lacked structure were seen to benefit most. The purpose of the residential care was to work with families and kids to return them home as soon as possible. It had to be local, community based and short term.

In addition to the TPs, the only other staff person who maintained an office at the home (on the side of the house where the family resided) was a therapist who worked regular daytime hours. A consultant who worked with the TPs was not located on site but maintained regular communication and held several meetings with the TPs during the week. The consultant answered to the actual head of homes who administered several programmes and only occasionally visited The Keys, while the therapist answered to a clinical director who served all programmes operated by the parent agency. Part time substitute house parents filled in for the TPs to allow time for vacations and week-ends off.

The first impression of The Keys was of a typical middle-class family home that bore little resemblance to the secure dorm facility environment of Brown House. During most of the day and night, the TPs and their children lived with and interacted with the resident girls. The TPs had personal and quiet time with their families and took occasional week-end trips, but they insisted that they responded to the girls in the group setting in the same way they did to their own children. The TPs believed in letting their kids 'blend in' with their own families. They used the same techniques on their own children (without the point system), and stressed that the expectations were the same: this 'had to be' because if they treated their own kids differently, the Keys residents would pick up on the inconsistency and the programme would not work.

All children in residence played together, watched TV, did homework in the living room or den or read and completed lessons in their bedrooms. Resident children went on planned, structured outings with the house staff or with substitute parents. The girls shared bunkbeds except for the oldest resident who was given her own room.

## The structure of the two homes

In Florida there is no overarching national Statute such as the *Children Act* 1989 that explicitly governs or provides operating principles for programmes like The Keys or Brown House. Rather, there are various general state policies that define what administrators can and cannot do with regard to numbers accommodated, health and safety concerns, licensing and so forth. These policies, set by the Florida Department of Children and Families do not seem to provide the kind of specific guidance to administrators offered by the *Children Act* in Britain.

Two important structural features distinguished both of these otherwise very different establishments from their English counterparts. First, the treatment agenda of each home strictly 'programmed' the residents' day by establishing a tight schedule that allowed comparatively little free time. Second, both programmes were built around strict behavioural regimes which, while very different from each other, shared a primary emphasis on 'points' gained for positive responses and taken away for negative behaviour. As will be explained below, these components actually drove the culture - in a sense making for maximum 'concordance' - but making it difficult to distinguish the cultural responses of staff and young people from the behaviour that reflected the logic of the regime.

## The structure of Brown House

The formal structure of the Brown House programme was defined by staff roles, programme activities, treatment plans, a behavioural points system and a declining commitment to a therapeutic model of drug treatment. Brown House had been founded in the late 1970s as a drug treatment programme for young adults. It was based on a Synanon-type confrontational approach, involving peer 'haircuts', nightly readings of client transgressions of the day and the dishing out of punishments. This model was more or less adapted for adolescents but increasingly adopted a therapeutic community focus, albeit with a token economy overlay.

Like many Florida youth programmes, Brown House's mandate became confused and was adapted to attract a larger client base. Specifically, the programme had to accommodate far greater numbers of delinquent referrals in order to survive. Prior to the tenure of the current administrator, who had been on board less than a year at the beginning of the study, a previous administrator had tried to strengthen the points system which relied heavily on 'bookings' or assignment of penalties for rule violations. The present director was committed to maintaining a therapeutic community atmosphere and, aside from the points system, did not believe in other forms of discipline. The previous policy of never discharging anyone had created an atmosphere of frequent fights and intimidation and had resulted in a high rate of running away because 'the kids who really wanted to be there were afraid of the kids who wanted to make trouble'.

When the new director came in last year, he instituted a 'no violence' policy and quickly began discharging any resident caught fighting. About six boys were discharged during the first month of his tenure but the numbers declined dramatically once the young people got the message that the no fighting rule was serious.

There remained an emphasis on drug treatment, probably beyond that justified by the histories and drug involvement of residents. This emphasis was one topic of debate between new and older staff, because the latter focused what appeared to be inordinate amounts of attention on relatively minor drug use and linked a variety of behavioural and cognitive issues to this 'dependency'.

The director believed the current system of discipline and control was built primarily on positive reinforcement; he felt he had stabilised the house and that the 'peers were now in control'. He believed that the positive reinforcement helped 'avoid power struggles' because it did not put staff in the position of making kids do things. Rather, the challenge of the job (the magic as he called it) was finding ways to make activities appealing to kids without requiring that they did them; 'the trick is to get kids to want to do stuff on their own'. He gave an example of how new weight training equipment sat unused for the first three months of his tenure until he started using the weight equipment himself daily to get kids involved. Once he started, kids got interested and he ultimately had to form weight lifting clubs which required that boys signed up to join.

In the old system, house discipline was based completely on bookings: everything each kid had done that day was read out and the kids were assigned extra chores to work off negative points. Now, they relied primarily on positive reinforcement. For example, instead of listing what the kid had done wrong at the meetings, they discussed everything he did *right*. Currently, in the director's view, bookings were 'tied to the real world in that they relied heavily on fines; kids had to give up house money as penalties'. The most severe penalties were 'redlines' which were generally impossible to 'buy off' as could be done in the cases of other transgressions. Redlines generally resulted in extra days in treatment and loss of weekend passes. The emphasis in the director's view was now on rewarding behaviour that yielded privilege points. These helped residents move to higher status levels within the home, gain more unsupervised home privileges and eventually get their own room.

However, the point system continued to provide the primary focus of day-to-day interaction between residents and staff. While observations were inevitably limited in the dorm units, much of the conversation between staff and residents centred on negotiations for positive points that a resident felt were deserved or on arguments about why a resident was getting 'booked' for some behaviour he believed was not his fault. Interaction and discussion around points and bookings, in fact, extended through structured activities including recreational outings and other group activities; school sessions were the only place where points were clearly not a topic of discussion.

Outcomes, understood as the future adjustment of residents, such as being drug and crime-free, were not systematically tracked by the Brown House programme. The complexity of the referral and criminal/juvenile justice systems meant that few programmes kept data on what happened to their clients after termination. The only opportunity most programmes had to measure failure was when a client was returned to the programme because of a new offence, violation of community supervision or as a result of abuse. Many relapses or re-offences never became known to facility staff especially since some reoffenders were charged as adults.

Hence, the outcomes of interest to staff were primarily changes in the home itself and short-term changes in residents. Within the Brown House facility the director had several 'barometers' for measuring the success of his new approach to behaviour including the fact that there were fewer holes in the wall, due to kids regularly punching out parts of the panel, than when he began. Violence had essentially ceased and running away had all but stopped.

Improvements in short-term resident outcomes included concrete gains in academic skills (the programme operated a highly regarded school programme and most graduates showed significant advances) and better decision making skills and anger management. Retention and completion rates were also higher than before. In the director's view Brown House was successful in accomplishing the aims and should have as its fundamental goal providing residents with a 'benchmark' for stability and sobriety that they could look back to in later periods of difficulty.

In addition, there were more subtle indicators of changes in the focus of the facility that had potential for changing the relationship of adolescents to conventional support groups in the community. While the former Brown House programme, driven in part by the therapeutic community philosophies, was insular in its treatment emphasis, the new programme was visibly community focused. The new director, in fact, argued that treatment was the least important part of the job of staff. The most important was to bring the community in and gain public support in an effort to establish connections between residents and conventional adults while changing the image of residents through community service and other ventures.

While family connections and family involvement were a problem for this programme, as they are in many UK homes, the emphasis on linkage with the outside world, if it caught on in a meaningful way, promised to change the focus of Brown House from a rather isolated treatment programme to a more dynamic feature of the community.

## The Structure of the Keys

Even more than in Brown House, staff and resident interaction in The Keys was dominated by the points system. The teaching parent model called for virtually constant feedback to children about their behaviour and style of interaction. While there was less programmed activity of the Brown House variety, there was much more programmed interaction between adult staff and children routinely throughout the day. In fact, on visits to the home it was rare during waking hours to find an occasion when one of the parents was not involved in a one-on-one encounter with one of the girls.

These encounters were not necessarily negative or focused on disciplining the child. Rather, they were seen, in the vernacular of the model, as 'teaching moments'. They were, however, focused on negotiations about points, especially from the child's perspective. The intensity of this constant teaching more than anything else distinguished The Keys from a normal family. Whether negative or when intended to grant privileges, feedback had to be immediate. The model placed great importance on 'rationales' given to kids to explain why following adults' instruction was in their best interest. Rationales had to be brief and to the point otherwise they became lectures. Praise was vitally important but it needed to be concise and sincere. A lasting and disturbing impression gained from the research observations was that without this constant programmed interchange, there would have been uncontrolled chaos and disruption in what was generally an orderly and pleasant home.

This response and the regime itself were based on a comprehensive national model of residential care for emotionally disturbed youth. A requirement for the job of house parent was demonstrated commitment to and competency in the model. Following a careful screening process, there was extensive pre-service training for TPs and ongoing in-service training and evaluation. Although TPs did not need to have professional qualifications, the training and evaluation system were well organised and professional.

The model itself, along with the close team relationships that TPs were expected to maintain with the therapist and the consultant (daily contact and meetings several times weekly) provided a great deal of structure. The written materials contained not only policy but also principles and values that TPs were expected to internalise. The concordance between the goals of the home and the views of the TPs was indicated by the fact that when asked about the purpose of residential care, both repeated the goals of The Keys almost in the words of the director – 'intermediate intervention to stabilise the youth and the family in order to return them to the home as soon as possible'.

Regarding outcomes, the director maintained that about 80% of residents completed the programme and that about 80% of those stayed out of the system for at least a year (the normal time of follow-up). Staff believed they were successful but generally maintained relatively low expectations because they knew that the children had often failed before. 'Success' was therefore often defined as a girl 'making good progress or co-operating' when she had previously created havoc and had constantly run away. In the eyes of the therapist, who believed that many residents were a difficult group as they had been homeless for extended periods before admission to the programme, 'success' in The Keys meant that a young resident did not 'go back out on the street'.

The success of the model itself had some support from research. A difficulty, however, was in transferring the teaching parent skills to real families and foster parents who may have little time or ability to provide the constant feedback and reinforcement that seemed capable of moulding behaviour in this somewhat artificial environment.

## Cultures in the two homes

The significance of the structures described was that their influence on staff and, to a somewhat lesser extent, resident behaviour was so strong that it was difficult to distinguish cultural features as being independent. Specifically, staff and child/youth responses in the programmes were far more driven by scheduled activities that were supposed to occupy the time of residents. Where these activities ended, staff and youth responses were based on the economy of points that became currency for purchasing privileges or avoiding punishment.

These two features of the programmes, in other words, simply did not allow sufficient discretion to permit full development of an independent youth or staff cultural response. It proved difficult to identify manifestations of responses that were not assumed by the logic of the system or the rules of daily participation in activities. In this sense, there was clearly 'concordance' between structure and culture because the regime of the two homes was the culture.

This is not to say that the researchers did not find an organisational culture in the homes. Rather, it is to say that cultural responses to various incidents were more often oppositional reactions that constituted rule violations, or at least reactions that suggested attitudes and beliefs inconsistent with policy. When staff physically or verbally abused residents, for example, or when residents abused each other, there was often a culture that supported this behaviour. There was little doubt that there were also oppositional resident cultures within each home (and oppositional staff cultures in one) but because these were clearly illicit, they were difficult to observe.

A second way that staff culture came into play in these highly regimented programmes was when staff simply did not understand or simply refused to implement management policy in accordance with the spirit of the regime. In both programmes, for example, managers held strong visions based on certain values about child and youth care. The behavioural regime for these managers was simply a means towards the end of providing opportunities for youth to practise and learn good decision making skills. However, in both homes, the regime used to provide this structure became an end in itself. It was, therefore, again difficult to observe cultural responses to situations that could be easily distinguished from the logic of behavioural structure. Examples of responses and their relationship to policy and the behavioural regime are included below.

## Cultures in Brown House

Relatively limited staff interactions observed in Brown House centred around bookings. Youths were often heard negotiating in order not to lose points or to gain them, and staff were in turn observed using points to control behaviour and (in their view) prevent disruption and aggressive incidents. From the residents' perspective, this was because getting through the programme, moving from one level to another, gaining privileges associated with each level and ultimately getting out of the programme required points. In between the intake and exit from the programme, status and rewards - a private room, longer home visits - could only be obtained by getting positive bookings and avoiding negative ones.

In this context the staff cultural response was difficult to detect. While among the counsellors there were noticeably individual styles used in interactions with individual residents, there were few opportunities for a common group response to the situations listed in Appendix Three, especially when there were only two counsellors on a shift at any given time. A strong common commitment to education and encouraging youth to increase academic performance were shared values, but these were again rewarded or penalised by staff (with the exception of the teacher) almost exclusively through points. At most, there were slightly oppositional subcultures that seemed to coalesce among some of the professionally qualified staff and the milieu counsellors. These centred around a greater commitment to the drug treatment mission than the current director was willing to promote. For residents, this often resulted in more emphasis on drug issues than might have been needed; for clinical staff it resulted in long assessment and progress reports focused on so-called addictive behaviour.

The administrator clearly held strong values about youth programming and articulated principles that could have formed the basis for a strong and positive staff culture. His vision was one that implied such a culture and his non-directive empowering management style (an approach affirmed by even those staff who did not share his philosophy) created a climate in which a strong staff culture could have flourished. However, aside from the shared value around education and rewarding and encouraging good performance, there appeared to be few easily identifiable shared staff values. And, although the administrator was actively attempting to minimise the importance of the point system in favour of a value-based response, it was apparent that for milieu counsellors the point system had essentially become the culture. Wider values and principles about how staff should interact with residents did not appear to be communicated to staff and maintaining the point regime for all practical purposes got in the way of this communication. Hence, there was a lack of concordance between the values and principles of the administrator and those of the line staff.

In the case of residents, although the fighting and youth-on-youth physical and verbal abuse, common under the previous administration had ceased, there was no doubt some remnant of the oppositional youth culture. It was, however, more under the surface than before. The director was correct in his frequent assertion that the peers in Brown House exercised a great deal of control over any aberrant behaviour of residents, presenting a situation manifest in the case of a united front against fighting. However, it was again difficult to separate this group response from the individual desire to gain or avoid losing points. On the positive side, general demeanour and civility had become an expectation that could be labelled cultural. However, because residents knew they were rewarded for certain behaviours, forms of communication and interaction styles, these could not be easily disentangled from the points system. Perhaps because these were older delinquent males, rituals around birthdays, holidays and parental visits were not apparent.

## The culture at The Keys

There was virtually perfect concordance between staff culture and the teaching parent regime in The Keys. This is again to say that cultural responses were difficult to distinguish. This was in part because there were only two staff and in part because the job itself required that TPs demonstrate their immersion in the values and principles of the model. As one of the TPs answered when asked what her role or principal task was, 'to implement the treatment plan... recognising the 'target areas'... teaching success in the family structure and after... teaching more advanced skills'. TPs hoped to build up young people's self-esteem, 'so they can envision a future; many of the kids cannot see a future for themselves because their self-esteem is so low'. When asked how much she valued her own role, one TP noted that 'the model is not based on personality'. She went on to say that the model does not work well unless staff can implement it 'in a natural way'. From what she said and from observations of her encounters with the girls, this required a great deal of patience as well as a nurturing and a warm disposition.

The model provided a protocol for virtually all situations listed in Appendix Three and those not addressed were covered by regulatory policy. Staff responses to anti-social behaviour which were frequently observed were simply not cultural or even group responses. For example, one teaching parent typically handled most instances one-on-one, with more severe incidents handled by isolating the youth from the other children for a brief period. Only the therapist dealt with issues in the group and this response was less dictated by culture than by her clinical training and desire to remain true to the treatment approach.

On the children's side, The Keys' residents certainly appeared to share a distinctive culture based on mutual respect, politeness and deference to adults. For example, the girls greeted visitors, asked if they would like refreshments, sought permission to leave the room or join in a game. They did chores together and assisted with preparing meals and clean-up duties. They sat at the kitchen table for all meals, practised excellent table etiquette and talked about their day at school when asked. It was very difficult to conclude, however, that these shared repertoires were anything other than programmed behaviours. Each resident would have been rewarded and reinforced for such behaviours since the first day in residence.

## Comparisons: Applying the Model in the USA

The choice of two programmes structured around behavioural, token economy regimes was in this regard limiting because less 'space' or discretion were allowed for cultural responses to take hold among staff or residents. The methodology, including the response indicators in Appendix Three, could perhaps have been applied more directly in less behaviourally-oriented therapeutic community programmes. It is also worth considering whether or not a slightly modified methodology and slightly different set of indicators could also be fashioned for programmes like Brown House and The Keys. One good reason for this is that such programmes are very common in the U.S.

To study cultural responses in such programmes might require more intensive ethnographic study. On the other hand, the list of key events in Appendix Three might be changed to include incidents more common to U.S. programmes for adolescents. Another interesting line of investigation might be to pursue the extent to which staff really do share a set of values that influences the way they use the points system or similar token economies.

These highly regimented models are, in part, one way that managers attempt to address the question raised in the Structure and Culture study about how they might establish concordance between structural goals and staff cultures. The managers would probably argue that such regimes are the only way to manage what would otherwise be chaos and disruption (especially as homes which lack these regimes, at least in South Florida, are often the most disruptive). It is also possible that funding agencies favour these approaches because, compared to some youth programmes in Florida which lack such structure and where negative staff and youth cultures are dominant, these programmes are low risk.

Managers who adopt these approaches are choosing not to let culture emerge naturally but in return may be getting the concordance they want. This was clearly true in The Keys and might become the case for Brown House. Is structure imposed by this kind of regimentation sufficient to generate positive staff and youth cultural responses or is it simply one of a number of obstacles, like some of those found in the UK homes, that restrict these responses and so limit their potentially valuable effects?

The clear difference between the two American homes and the nine British ones described in the research is the significance of regime. In the British context, the parameters are set by The *Children Act* 1989 which guarantees a welfare oriented approach. The formal goals are the decisions and processes by which these societal goals are implemented and concordance is only achieved if the belief goals held by staff are also complementary. Thus, there are three components that need to be mutually supportive. In the American context, the formal goals are more significant. They have to incorporate societal expectations and are likely to be reinforced by the strong beliefs of managers. Control over what happens in the homes is less by legislation and Government issued guidance and more by established treatment approaches scrutinised by fellow professionals. The regime is the 'be all and end all' in this situation whereas it is only one of three components in the British homes. This also explains why the American homes appear more treatment oriented even though the tasks are similar.

# Appendix 6: Principles underpinning the *Children Act*, 1989

The discussion in Chapter Ten showed that detailed work is required to establish the societal, formal and belief goals of a residential home. Certain aids can help, the most important of which is *The Care of Children: Principles and Practice in Regulations and Guidance* (HMSO, 1989). This sets out the principles that underpin the *Children Act*, 1989 and Volume Four of the guidance.

Forty-two principles are discussed and these are laid out below. (The number of the principle in the publication is given in brackets). They have been divided into three groups: those concerned with perspectives that inform practice; those concerned with the quality of services and those focusing in the effects of intervention. The first category is sub-divided into principles and processes and the second into ensuring good quality and making good decisions.

A    **Perspectives that inform practice**
1    *Principles that underpin good practice*

Children and young people and their parents should all be considered as individuals with particular needs and potentialities. (1)

Although some basic needs are universal, there can be a variety of ways of meeting them. (2)

Admission to public care by virtue of a compulsory order is itself a risk to be balanced against others. So also is the accommodation of a child by a local authority. (8)

Corporate parenting is not 'good enough' on its own. (22)

In carrying out the duties and responsibilities laid upon them in legislation and regulations, local authorities should put into practice the principles of good work with children and families. (27)

Agencies have special, parental responsibilities for the minority of children who are in long-term out-of-home placements. (33)

When alternatives are being considered and/or decisions made, certain individuals or groups may need to be involved. (34)

Services to vulnerable children have to be largely provided through those who give them day to day care whether these are parents, relatives, residential social workers or foster carers. In each case, a balance must be struck between offering carers support (thus building confidence) and holding them accountable for the child's well-being. (35)

Agencies have a responsibility to support placements which they have made. (39)

Co-operation between organisations, departments and individuals is crucial in the provision of protection for vulnerable children and also in ensuring proper use of available resources. (41)

2    *Getting the process right*

Caregivers - whether parents, foster carers or residential staff - need both practical resources and a feeling of being valued if they are to give of their best. (36)

Appropriate training should be provided for carers. (37)

There should be machinery for resolving differences of view or minor disputes, e.g. through involvement of a team leader, fostering officer or other appropriate individual or through re-negotiating written agreements at the request of any of the signatories. (38)

Registers and records must be maintained and kept up to date. (40)

Foster homes and residential establishments used for the placement of children should be reviewed at regular and suitable intervals though this needs to be done sensitively so as to avoid undermining carers' confidence or making children feel insecure. (42)

**B**    **Quality of services**

*1*    *Ensuring good quality care*

Children are entitled to protection from neglect, abuse and exploitation. (3)

There are unique advantages for children in experiencing normal family life in their own birth family and every effort should be made to preserve the child's home and family links. (5)

Parents are individuals with needs of their own. (6)

The development of a working partnership with parents is usually the most effective route to providing supplementary or substitute care for their children. (7)

When out-of-home care is necessary, active steps should be taken to ensure speedy return home. (11)

Parents should be expected and enabled to retain their responsibilities and to remain as closely involved as is consistent with their child's welfare, even if that child cannot live at home either temporarily or permanently. (12)

Siblings should not be separated when in care or when being looked after under voluntary arrangements unless this is part of a well thought out plan based on each child's needs. (13)

Family links should be actively maintained through visits and other forms of contact. Both parents are important even if one of them is no longer in the family home and fathers should not be overlooked or marginalised. (14)

Wider families matter as well as parents - especially siblings and grandparents. (15)

Continuity of relationships is important, and attachments should be respected, sustained and developed. (16)

Change of home, caregiver, social worker or school almost always carries some risk to a child's development and welfare. (17)

Time is a crucial element in child care and should be reckoned in days and months rather than years. (18)

Since discrimination of all kinds is an everyday reality in many children's lives, every effort must be made to ensure that agency services and practices do not reflect or reinforce it. (21)

Children's long-term welfare must be protected by prompt, positive and pro-active attention to the health and education of those in both short and long-term care. (24)

Young people's wishes must be elicited and taken seriously. (25)

As young people grow up, preparation for independence is a necessary and important part of the parental role which child care agencies carry for young people in long-term care. (26)

The various departments of a local authority (e.g. health, housing, education and social services) should co-operate to provide an integrated service and range of resources even when such co-operation is not specifically required by law. (28)

The twin issues of confidentiality and access to records need to be addressed by all local authorities and child care organisations. (29)

Caregivers are entitled to have appropriate information about any child or young person placed in their charge and have a duty to keep this confidential. (30)

Letters and documents which are sent to parents and young people should be written in language which is fully comprehensible to them. (31)

Planning is a crucial responsibility for all agencies providing services to children and their families. (32)

2.  *Making good decisions*

A child's age, sex, health, personality, race, culture and life experiences are all relevant to any consideration of needs and vulnerability and have to be taken into account when planning or providing help. (4)

If young people cannot remain at home, placement with relatives or friends should be explored before other forms of placement are considered. (9)

If young people have to live apart from their family of origin, both they and their parents should be helped to consider alternatives and contribute to the making of an informed choice about the most appropriate form of care. (10)

C      **Producing good outcomes**

Every young person needs to develop a secure sense of personal identify and all those with parental or caring responsibilities have a duty to offer encouragement and support in this task. (19)

All children need to develop self-confidence and a sense of self-worth, so alongside the development of identity, and equally important is self-esteem. (20)

Young people should not be disadvantaged or stigmatised by action taken on their behalf, e.g. as a result of admission to care or to special residential provision. (23)

# Index

 dartington **social research** series

This book is one of a series dealing with aspects of what is beginning to be known as a common language for the personal social services. The aims is to build up knowledge about different groups of children in need in a form that will be readily understood by policy makers, professionals, researchers and consumers and so make it possible to predict outcomes for such children and to design an effective agency response.

MAKING RESIDENTIAL CARE WORK concentrates on aspects of the process of supporting children in need. It considers the relationship between the different objectives for organisations sheltering these children–what are called the structural goals–and proposes a relationship between them and the culture of residential centres. As with nearly all Dartington studies, it considers the effects this variable equation has on outcome, both for the organisations looking after the children and for the children themselves. The terms defined in the book have subsequently been used to frame and analyse the results from other Dartington studies and some local authorities have begun to use the ideas to fashion more effective services.

The language of the personal social services is evolving. It is making use of the results from Dartington studies, of practical developments properly evaluated in a number of test sites and other findings from other groups working in the area. Comment from those making policy, managing services, working directly with children and families or receiving help from personal social service agencies is always welcome. There is a website describing the evolution of the common language at **www.dsru.co.uk** and a series of related papers is available from the Dartington Unit at Warren House, Warren Lane, Dartington, Totnes, Devon, TQ9 6EG email **unit@dsru.co.uk** and Fax +44-1803-866783.